CHRISTIANITY
— THE OTHER POLITICAL PARTY —
THE HIJACKING OF A FAITH

PASTOR OWEN E. WILLIAMS

Christianity: The Other Political Party
Copyright © 2025 by Pastor Owen E. Williams

All rights reserved. No part of this book may be used or reproduced by any means, graphic, electronic, or mechanical, including photocopying, recording, taping or by any information storage retrieval system without the written permission of the author except in the case of brief quotations embodied in critical articles and reviews.

Cover Concept Design: Pastor Owen E. Williams
Cover Design: Marko Polic of 99designs by Vista
Typesetting: Edge of Water Designs, edgeofwater.com

ISBNs:
979-8-218-70491-9 (Paperback)
979-8-218-71349-2 (eBook)

Publisher: OE Williams Ministries
oewilliamsministries.com/books

DEDICATION

First, I must thank my heavenly Father for the wonderful things he has done.

To my Family, my wife of thirty-five years, Elder Debora Williams, for her love, continued support, and daily prayer over my life. And my daughter, who is the joy of my life.

Elder Debora has been the lead servant of the powerful "Desire a Prayer Life Ministries" for the last twenty-three years. God has anointed Elder Debora with a ministry that allows her to bring the "Power of Prayer" back into the home and to help people develop a disciplined prayer life at www.desireaprayerlife.com.

To my precious daughter, Desiree Rose Williams, who has matured into a beautiful and responsible young woman over the last decade, your dad loves you more than words can express and is deeply proud of you.

My mother and father's memories, as well as their

love and guidance, continue to inspire me and shape the words of this book.

ACKNOWLEDGEMENTS

I am deeply and sincerely grateful to the following individuals whose unwavering support and belief in my work have made this book a reality and testament to the power of collective effort. Your unique contributions, whether big or small, have been invaluable. Sincerely, I would like to express my sincere gratitude for your unwavering support and faith in me and this project.

To my Lord and Savior Jesus Christ, your presence in my life has been more than a guiding light. It has been the essence of my existence, shaping the very words of this book. Despite my many sins and faults, your forgiveness and grace continue to shape my life according to your divine will. I am forever and sincerely grateful for your love and mercy.

And to you, dear reader, I am thankful for your time and interest in my work. Your presence in this journey has been instrumental in the success of this book.

I am eternally grateful to my beloved wife and life partner of thirty-five years, whose continued love, support, and encouragement have been a constant source of strength. To my daughter, you continue to fill my heart with pride and joy. To my sister, Susan Watkins, there is no better sister in the world. Your love, phone calls, and retirement vision mean the world to me. I love you dearly. To my mother and father, who have both returned to the Lord, I am grateful for the trials and struggles you endured to keep our family together. To my nieces and nephews, your love is endless and precious to me, and I am grateful for every one of you.

To the St. Mark Missionary Baptist Church, there is no place I would serve God other than with you. You are all incredible.

PREFACE

The Christian faith is barely recognizable today compared to its foundational doctrines and beliefs as outlined in the Bible. Biblical teachings on bias, partiality, indifference, and warnings of greed, lust, and the love of money seem foreign to today's Christian church.

This body of the faithful is no longer content with even having a form of godliness. It only displays a consuming gospel of selfishness, hate, separatism, violence, racial identity, stubborn lies, vengefulness, privilege, and entitlement. This loud and bold body takes excellent pride in prognosticating and pontificating these behaviors while demonstrating zero faith in the "Ancient of Days," who says that our lives are "but a vapor in the wind." There seems to be extraordinarily little understanding of seasons and the ability to transition and adapt to God's will when he does something new in the land. Blinded by desire and enslaved to the flesh, this body seems incapable of brotherly love, personal charity towards the stranger, living justly, having mercy, and walking humbly before their God. And, in this ethos, they have inflicted much pain and suffering amongst the brethren.

But like the apostle Paul, I see another member in the body taking control, confusing the mind, manipulating the flesh, and rendering us blind to our behaviors. In this blindness, we have switched faithfulness to God for patriotism to the country, commitment to submission, repentance, and the will of God for vengeance, separatism, racism, sexism, and sectarianism. Let us pray that God touches our eyes.

TABLE OF CONTENTS

Acknowlegements	v
Preface	vii
Introduction	xiii
Chapter 1: Current State	1
Old Doctrines Becoming New Realities	4
Dominion Theology	10
Reconstruction Theology	11
The Apostasy and Politics	15
Chapter 2: Western Hemisphere Christianity	19
God and the Gun	21
Gun Control and the Right to Bear Arms	22
Politics	25
Theology of Identity	28
Chapter 3: Religious or Imperialistic Conflicts	32
Israel's Assimilation	33
Judah's Captivity	34
Occupation	35
Crusades	40
The Ottoman Empire	42

Chapter 4: The Thoughts of Man	45
Magna Carta	46
The American Bill of Rights	48
The Constitution of the Fifth Republic	50
The Behavior of Man	52
Chapter 5: The Desires of Man	56
Desire Without Discipline	57
Sexual Lust	61
Love of Money	63
Love of Power	65
Love of Status: Pride	68
Affluence Vs. Influence	70
Chapter 6: The Rules of Man	74
Dangers of Elitism	75
Pride of Elitism	79
Sins of Elitism	81
Chapter 7: The Allure of Attention	83
Attention Seekers at Pandemic Levels	84
The Transmittance	90
Political Instigators	92
Radicalization	94

Chapter 8: The Appetite of Hate	96
Stages of Hate	98
Combating Hate	100
A Demonic Design	102
Chapter 9: Steps of a Demonic Design	104
To Steal	107
To Kill	108
To Destroy	109
Dismantling the Demonic Design	111
Capitalism: Satan's Playground	113
Chapter 10: A Look Back	119
Eyes That Do Not See	121
Divine Decree	123
A Reflection of Gratitude	125
Divine Right vs. Divine Law	128
Chapter 11: The Heavenly Vision: Restoration of The World	134
Humanity	139
Creation	146
Discipleship/Stewardship	150
Unity Through Love	151

Conclusion	154
Bibliography	157
More About Pastor Williams	158

INTRODUCTION

Today, we see an emboldened Christian nationalist doctrine espousing an ideology that has long been defunct and defeated but still lives on in the hearts and desires of a small global minority who are becoming successful in making this ideology a Christian grassroots political movement.

In the United States, this ideology has hijacked the Republican party and threatens to usher in a lawless population if their privilege and entitlement desires are not realized. These desires run the gamut from extreme financial conservative policies that have the potential to disenfranchise poor people who are predominantly black and brown with limited education. It has also become increasingly consumed and concerned with racial identity and citizenship.

On the other side of the political spectrum, the Democratic Party's ideologies have become increasingly irresponsible regarding sound fiscal management and distribution, and dangerously irresponsible in matters of accountability and responsibility concerning citizenship.

At the same time, both parties cite Christian values as the foundation for their love of country and fellow citizens. Who is right in their beliefs? Are both correct? Or are both wrong? Are the synoptic gospels big enough to accommodate both ideologies, and if so, how can they coexist?

This book explores these questions by examining how these phenomena came to be, their symptoms in the current American political climate, and the consequences should it continue to go unchecked. We, the faithful, can be reminded by God's Word and follow His heavenly vision to avoid these pitfalls of entwining Christianity and nationalism on a political scale.

Chapter 1
Current State

Ecclesiastes 9:18

Wisdom is better than weapons of war, but one sinner destroys much good.

In King Solomon's writings, he explores the theology of wisdom and the meaninglessness of life without God while simultaneously highlighting the limitations of human understanding. We find ourselves in highly adversarial times, and our advanced intellect and wisdom have failed to produce the greater societal peace we desire. Instead, we have increased our tribalism, mistrust, greed, and anger toward each other.

Politics and diplomacy were once noble and honorable professions, where individuals served according to their conscience, which in most cases was driven by a sense of obligation to do what was right and good. Oh, how we have fallen, but what is most dangerous about this fall is the acceptance of our fall. We are no longer ashamed to lie, to be hateful, to be vengeful, to be racist, to be separatist, to be afraid, to be silent, and to be willing.

Scripture teaches us that one sinner can destroy much good work. How often have we seen and witnessed a noble and honorable leader leave the world stage or the CEO position, only to be replaced by an ethically challenged one? And how many times have these challenged ones wrapped themselves in the holy scriptures and created religious and sectarian discord among the citizens?

The foundation of sin is moral corruption that desires to corrupt; morally corrupt leaders sow discord among people, create divisive environments, and make it almost impossible for civility to flourish. In the last seventy-five years, the United States of America has transformed from an apartheid political system to an infantile democracy to a potential autocracy and oligarchy.

The foundation of America's political doctrine has always been based on boss-ship. Like South Africa's apartheid political system, America's system was also built on institutions of separateness or institutional racial segregation that was maintained by an authoritarian political culture of boss-hood to preserve the melting pot's white majority rule. This system is founded on a culture of hierarchy, insecurity, anxiety, and repression. What is so unfortunate about this is that the gospels have been used as a political weapon and, ultimately, a political party to assist in preserving the past and bringing it into the future, and like then, we find reasonably intelligent, well-mannered leaders in and out of Gods Holy church willing and ready to assist, as they transform Christianity into the other political party.

The mission statement for this movement, known as MAGA, is summed up this way: America is a white Christian Nation enclosed by borders. Anyone within these borders should look like me, pray like me, and vote like me. MAGA stands for "Make America Great Again." It became the campaign slogan for the 2016 Republican presidential candidate. Many believe the phrase and its movement have a nefarious and duplicitous meaning and intent.

Old Doctrines Becoming New Realities

Since the election victories of President Barack Obama, a concerted and aggressive movement has risen in the United States and around the world to push back against misperceived threats to the white way of life, culture, and power. Due to this misguided perception, we see old doctrines resurrected from a time long past.

One hundred years ago, in the United States, following World War I, the world began to grow closer together through trade and commerce, facilitated by advancements in travel and immigration. This movement in America sought to revive traditional Christian values and establish a strict national system that excluded anything different from this limited and narrow interpretation of Christianity, blending it and ultimately transforming it into the political movement we see today. Scripture is noticeably clear about the consequences of going back to a sinful past, **Hebrews 10:26-27,** *"If we deliberately keep on sinning after we have received the knowledge of the truth, no sacrifice for sins is left, but only a fearful expectation of judgment and of raging fire that will consume the enemies of God."*

Isaiah 43:18-19, *"Forget the former things; do not dwell on the past. See, I am doing a new thing! Now it* *springs up; do you not perceive it? I am making a way in the wilderness and streams in the wasteland."*

These scriptures reveal a specific type of duplicity and nefariousness in the behavior of those who want to look back to an evil and sinful time and use the gospels as a political party and weaponize them.

Anyone spouting a separatist ideology in the United States, a country born out of immigrants from every country on the planet, is either quite misinformed of their history, has a hateful nature due to some trauma, feels entitled to have things that do not belong to them, or views their world through a racist perspective, or all of the above. The U.S. Congress has historically been on opposite sides of the spectrum between the Democratic and Republican parties; even though eighty-eight percent (88%) identify as Christians, this body still finds it exceedingly difficult to unite and serve, especially during the period between 2008 and 2024. Many claim to be called by God; only time can reveal whether these are authentic callings. Still, the evidence of someone's call is not based on or measured by a matrix of popularity, wealth, or achievement, but by the individual's consistent, humble faithfulness to that call, despite how unsuccessful it may initially appear. God puts a call on individuals' lives for them to fulfill the Christian mission, which is to be obedient to the following:

- Share their faith in word and deed.
- Constantly be involved in the ministry of help through service to others.
- Let others feel the love of Christ through acts of kindness, compassion, and charity.

The apostle Paul said God called him on the Damascus Road, and his calling would successfully measure his suffering for Christ.

2 Corinthians 11: 16-33, *"I repeat: Let no one take me for a fool. But if you do, tolerate me just as you would a fool, so that I may indulge in a bit of boasting. In this* *self-confident boasting, I am not talking as the Lord would but as a fool. Since many are boasting in the way the world does, I, too, will boast. You gladly put up with fools since you are so wise! You even put up with anyone who enslaves you, exploits you, takes advantage of you, puts on airs, or slaps you in the face. To my shame, I admit that we were too weak for that!*

Whatever anyone else dares to boast about—I am speaking as a fool—I also dare to brag about. Are they Hebrews? So am I. Are they Israelites? So am I. Are they Abraham's descendants? So am I. Are they servants of Christ? (I am out of my mind to talk like this.) I am more. I have worked much harder, been in prison more frequently, been flogged more severely, and been exposed to death again and again. Five times, I received from the Jews the forty lashes minus one. Three times, I was beaten with rods; once, I was pelted with stones; three times, I was shipwrecked; I spent a night and a day in the open sea, and I have been constantly on the move. I have been in danger from rivers, in danger from bandits, in danger from my fellow Jews, in danger from Gentiles; in danger in the city, in danger in the country, in danger at sea, and in danger from false believers. I have labored and toiled and have often gone without sleep; I have known hunger and thirst and have often gone without food; I have been cold and naked. Besides everything else, I face daily the pressure of my concern for all the churches. Who is weak, and I do not feel weak? Who is led into sin, and I do not inwardly burn? If I must, I will boast of the things that show my weakness. The God and Father of the Lord Jesus, who will be praised forever, knows I am not lying. In Damascus, the governor under King Aretas had been tasked with guarding the city of the Damascenes to arrest me. But I was lowered in a basket from a window in the wall and slipped through his hands."

The ultimate purpose of a calling is to show God's power and grace within a fallen, weak human vessel. The purpose of boasting is to point it all back to God, not to insinuate that you, the weak, fallen individual, are so good that you were chosen, and God needed you alone for this task. So, what qualifies us for a calling is not our greatness but rather our sinful weakness, and that is what we should be boasting about: our sinful weakness and the power of his might to clean, restore, and resurrect our lives.

Dominion Theology

Having dominion has been a foundational goal of most European and Western civilizations. Dominion theology is a movement that says God, through Christ, exercises dominion over this world and that believers, through their identification with Christ, have dominion over this world through obedience to God's commandments and faithful service. This theology holds that Christians will ultimately be regarded as the beneficiaries of this world.[1] This Theology becomes conflicted as it begins to lord over other Christians from different backgrounds, races, ethnicities, and genders, and violates the command

---

1   Paul Enns, The Moody Handbook Of Theology, (Moody Publishers, 2014), 546,547

of Christ that asks us not to lord over one another as the Gentiles/unbelievers do.

Reconstruction Theology

Unlike Dominion Theology, Christian Reconstruction Theology is a relatively recent philosophy that argues Christians have a moral obligation to reclaim every institution for the sake of Jesus Christ. This must be done through biblical law, with Christians reconstructing culture in every area of life, including education, medicine, agriculture, economics, personal occupations, politics, law enforcement, family life and relationships, church life, the arts, and the sciences.[2]

These views are interpreted from the scriptures:

Genesis 1:28, *"God blessed them and said to them, 'Be fruitful and increase in number; fill the earth and subdue it. Rule over the fish in the sea, the birds in the sky, and every living creature that moves on the ground."*

---

2   Ibid, 547

Genesis 9: 1-7, *"Then God blessed Noah and his sons, saying to them, 'Be fruitful and increase in number and fill the earth. The fear and dread of you will fall on all the beasts of the earth, the birds in the sky, every creature that moves along the ground, and all the fish in the sea; they are given into your hands. Everything that lives and moves about will be food for you. Just as I gave you the green plants, I now give you everything. But you must not eat meat with its lifeblood still in it. And for your lifeblood, I will surely demand an accounting. I will demand an accounting from every animal. And from each human being, too, I will demand an accounting for the life of another human being. Whoever sheds human blood, by humans shall their blood be shed; for in the image of God has God made humanity. As for you, be fruitful and increase in number; multiply on the earth and increase upon it.'"*

In these scriptures, many babes in Christ are manipulated into developing deep resentment toward the world and its things, including its people. Here is where you can find all manner of oppression, the domination of women, privilege for a select few, and unfair distributions of resources. God's word is pure, holy, and trustworthy. Man's heart and mind are limited, unholy, and easily manipulated to lie. God has called us through Jesus Christ first to be holy, then faithful in living and loving on this earth, to unify and not divide or judge.

The ongoing problem within the Christian faith is interpretation. Christianity is a religion that fosters a relationship with Jesus Christ; this relationship is accompanied by an established framework designed to develop us into holy, loving, and more resilient individuals, resisting sin. The more we separate ourselves from sin, the closer we draw to Christ, and the closer we draw to Christ, the more revelation we receive about Christ and ourselves. For this process to occur, sinners must completely surrender and submit their hearts and wills to God. This means trusting him with our fears, rage, and anxieties.

But this is not what is happening in our current

Christian nationalist movement, for it is a mixture of Christian nationalism, venture capitalism, corporate barons, and the super-rich wrapping themselves in a cloak of concern-patriotism and loving Christianity. That produces the most offensive and evil type of tormentor. C.S. Lewis, the British Anglican Theologian and literary scholar, said this about this type of tormentor. ***"Of all tyrannies, a tyranny sincerely exercised for the good of its victims may be the most oppressive. Living under robber barons rather than omnipotent moral busybodies would be better. The robber baron's cruelty may sometimes sleep, and his cupidity may sometimes be satiated, but those who torment us for our good will torment us without end, for they do so with the approval of their conscience."***

Today's tormentors torment with the belief that you are much better off in your life if they maintain their positions of wealth, entitlement, power, and privilege, and they are the ones who determine how much of the pie you will have throughout your life.

The Apostasy and Politics

Matthew 24:12-13, *"And because lawlessness will abound, the love of many will grow cold. But he who endures to the end shall be saved."*

Many believers will eventually repudiate Christ and outright rebel against the teachings of the gospels. Scripture describes this period as the "apostasy," a great time of falling away. This crisis does not occur in a vacuum but rather represents a slow and consistent erosion of the guardrails and boundaries of morality and accountability.

2 Timothy 3:1-5, *"But know this, that in the last days perilous times will come: For men will be lovers of themselves, lovers of money, boasters, proud, blasphemers, disobedient to parents, unthankful, unholy, unloving, unforgiving, slanderers, without self-control, brutal, despisers of good, traitors, headstrong, haughty, lovers of pleasure rather than lovers of God, having a form of godliness but denying its power. And from such people turn away!"*

Humanity has always been at odds with God, with many finding the Judeo-Christian faith too restrictive and the Islamic faith too repressive. The question of our times is, "Is the concept of God relevant in modern and technologically advanced societies?" Statistical data show that many younger generations worldwide are loosely associated with some form of faith. Still, the majority reject the traditional, structured manner of Sunday morning church attendance.

The reasons for this shift are multifaceted; the resistance to the structure is a big part of it, the youth's perspective of the restrictiveness of faith does not fit well into the creativity and carefreeness of the younger generation's lifestyles, and the biggest reason is the technology which provides headline news information in real-time no matter where in the world it is happening. This includes the behavior of the church and its leaders. This last part is the easiest one to turn around, as it relates to the hypocrisy and viciousness of the saints. The thing about biblical prophecy is that it is a guaranteed certainty based on the nature of the human heart.

2 Thessalonians 2:1-4, *"Concerning the coming of our Lord Jesus Christ and our being gathered to him, we ask you, brothers and sisters, not to become easily unsettled or alarmed by the teaching allegedly from us whether by a prophecy or by word of mouth or by letter asserting that the day of the Lord has already come. Do not let anyone deceive you in any way, for that day will not come until the rebellion occurs and the man of lawlessness is revealed, the man doomed to destruction. He will oppose and exalt himself over everything called God or is worshiped, so that he sets himself up in God's temple, proclaiming himself to be God."*

Hebrews 6: 4-6, *"It is impossible for those who have once been enlightened, who have tasted the heavenly gift, who have shared in the Holy Spirit, who have tasted the goodness of the word of God and the powers of the coming age and who have fallen away, to be brought back to repentance. To their loss, they are crucifying*

the Son of God all over again and subjecting him to public disgrace."

Among us, there are attention seekers who will use any and everything at their disposal to satisfy their insatiable appetite and feed this desire, even by blaspheming God's Holy Church by using the bad behavior of its members. The danger in this dynamic is that the attention seekers will tell you they are correct in pointing out church hypocrisy, and even if this is true, they are dead wrong in believing and proclaiming that the bad behavior of a saint who is a sinner saved by grace, is because the faith is terrible itself.

This thinking is like blaming a parent for their grown children's criminal behavior. It cannot be done because of these two words: Accountability and Responsibility. Every adult, at some point in their life, must accept accountability and responsibility for their actions and decisions. Sooner rather than later.

Chapter 2

WESTERN HEMISPHERE CHRISTIANITY

Genesis 9:6

Whoever sheds man's blood, by man his blood shall be shed, for in the image of God. He made man. And as for you, be fruitful and multiply; Bring forth abundantly in the earth and multiply in it.

Matthew 5:9

Blessed are the peacemakers, for they shall be called the sons of God

CHRISTIANITY: THE OTHER POLITICAL PARTY

As Christianity migrated to the Americas through Spain, England, and France's exploration activities, it brought violence and brutality to the shores of the Indigenous peoples who had yet to recover from it to this present day. In my fourth book, "American Christianity, Black Liberation, White Legalism," I explored that journey from the perspective of the oppressed and the oppressor. I found out that Christianity practiced in the West has degraded from its original status.

Now, this degradation is due to the character of Christians who arrived on these shores and their true motivations for coming. For as many missionaries who witnessed and preached the gospel of Jesus Christ to the Indigenous peoples of the North American continent, there were an equal number of newcomers who brutally and violently took and killed to satisfy their lustful desires that ruled the human heart. This is the psychological dynamic and dilemma that human beings face, eloquently described by the Apostle Paul in his letter to the Romans, chapter 7.

Romans 7:18-19, *"For I know that in me (that is, in my flesh) nothing good dwells; for to will is present with me, but how to perform what is good I do not find. For the good that I will do, I do not do; but the evil I will not do, that I practice."*

God and the Gun

Spain, England, and France may have explored America, but it was conquered and built by Smith & Wesson, Colt, and Remington. We have always had an innate fascination with guns and their life-taking power. This fascination has been enshrined in our constitution in the Second Amendment, which guarantees us the right to bear arms. Gun statistics generally claim that two-thirds of U.S. adults say they own a gun.

This fascination is now displayed in God's Holy Church by His appointed and anointed pastors. Not to be misleading, there are some very sound and good reasons for the rise of guns in churches. Due to the increase in fatal shootings at houses of worship, many churches are using armed security as well as arming the congregation as a security measure.

What makes this even more dangerous is when church pastors and leaders expand perceived threats to not only the gunman at the door but also other faiths, political ideologies, cultural differences, and races in the name of a Christian Army. Sometimes, an issue, cause, or emotion can be so consuming that we do not even realize it when we have deviated from our true path or calling.

Gun Control and the Right to Bear Arms

Every person born of a woman has an absolute right to live in peace and security, whether financial, emotional, or physical. *(Luke 22:36, "Let him who has no sword sell his mantle and buy one.")* Gun control has become a very emotionally charged and consuming debate in our society, as it seems to limit the Second Amendment as to who can own a gun, how many guns, and what types of firearms. One side believes it is an absolute, constitutionally guaranteed right, while the other feels a measure of public safety and government responsibility must be included.

Most people are confused about how this has become a matter of ecclesiastical policy. Christ plainly states that people have a divine right to self-defense and should also have a right to own a weapon for self-defense. Today's question, central to this current debate, is who has this right and who does not. We can all agree that toddlers of a certain age should not have this right; next could be people convicted of felony crimes like murder, attempted murder, armed robbery, and so forth.

Interestingly, through the Magisterium Council of bishops and in consultation with the Pope, the Roman Catholic Church has yet to issue any statements or decrees regarding firearms as part of its church polity and the laity's responsibilities within the congregation. The Magisterium is the sole official and supreme authority in the Catholic Church responsible for bringing about change. From 1962 to 1965, the Magisterium conducted the "Second Vatican Council," also known as Vatican II. This council led to the emergence of global ecumenical ministries and cooperation with Protestantism, marking a significant reversal of centuries of Catholic beliefs and behaviors.

In contrast, Protestant churches throughout the United States of America have made gun ownership a divine and constitutional right of self-defense, not just individual self-defense but also political, patriotic, and patriarchal. These ministries are found in more rural and suburban communities throughout the midwestern and southern states.

As previously mentioned, what makes this so dangerous is the misguided perception of who the enemies at the gate are. These groups typically identify politically with the Republican party and, lately, with the Christian Coalition and MAGA wings of that party, and identify their enemies as Democrats, Liberals, Progressives, Immigrants, and any group challenging their misperceived authority. This dangerous mindset tends to bring division within the "Body of Christ" through competition and entitlement behavior.

This belief system perverts the foundational doctrine of the Christian faith, which is built upon "God so loved the world that He gave His only begotten Son that whoever believes in Him shall not perish but have eternal life" to "God loves me, my race, my political party, and my country and gives us eternal life." This misguided belief triggers a misguided backlash from most minority Christian communities, further dividing the body of Christ. The backlash could have been triggered by an intentional provocation to a sinful time in our country filled with all manner of atrocities and a strong desire to never return to or be subjugated to that ever again. These communities can be very traumatized by these provocations, leaving them in need of a cathartic moment to purify their thoughts and behaviors.

Politics

In the United States, an even more significant issue than

guns that encompasses both Christian ideology and political legality is the abortion issue. It is an issue not only of our times but also the one primarily responsible for the rise of the "Christian Right", a movement that went somewhat dormant for the last sixty years as a dominant political movement and has now become a political party.

The Christian Right emerged in the late 1970s, when Rev. Jerry Falwell and other Christian leaders encouraged Christian congregations to become involved in local and national politics. Their foundational grievances were the restoration of school prayer and the rights of the unborn. They found a home in the Republican Party with the election of President Reagan. They formed alliances with the Moral Majority, the Christian Coalition, Focus on the Family, and the American Center for Law & Justice.

All these groups fall under the MAGA coalition today. They have been successful in electing President Trump twice to the Presidency, who, in turn, was able to appoint conservative Supreme Court Justices who overturned Roe Vs Wade after fifty years of standing precedent. Overturning a constitutional right is a lot easier than making its replacement popular; this requires an overwhelming campaign of negativity directed at the replaced "Right" and the demonization of its supporters.

Ever since the close 2000 Presidential election between President George W. Bush and Vice-President Al Gore, all future presidential elections have become increasingly more divisive, abusive in nature, and characterized by rancor and character assassination between candidates. This behavior culminated in the 2020 presidential election, in which President Trump refused to concede and initiate the peaceful transfer of power. This led to the January 6th insurrection at the United States Capitol building, aimed at stopping the peaceful transfer of power. These events started with a lie, and the political machine that sold it to an unsuspecting public who listened to the lies twenty-four hours a day, seven days a week.

Theology of Identity

These issues of divisiveness are often exacerbated by how we identify ourselves, "I am a Republican" or "I am a Democrat," in an all-or-nothing manner. And it's not just in politics. In our society today, identity dominates every aspect of human life, especially when dealing with the LGBTQ community. All people demand the rights of recognition and representation. However, identity is self-constructed; people create themselves to be what they feel most comfortable being.

In Knowing God, J.I. Packer discusses the numerous benefits of knowing God. Brian Rosner built on this topic in *Known by God*. I believe that today, we are highly consumed with making others see us, where we come from, who we are, and how we love and pray. We have lost sight of the fact that it is better to be known by people for our character and moral behavior than to make them understand who we are.

The difference is that identity is not displayed solely in desires but through character, faith, morality, commitment, kindness, and brotherly love. God told the prophet Jeremiah that before he was in his mother's womb, He knew him and ordained him a prophet to the nation.

Jeremiah 1:5, *"Before I formed you in the womb, I knew you. Before you were born, I sanctified you; I ordained you a prophet to the nations."*

Some like to think that this scripture speaks to the pre-existent nature of God's call on our lives, but that does not explain the theology of internal sin. This scripture primarily addresses free will, individual decisions, and ultimate destinations. Let us think about that for a minute. However, Jeremiah revealed his righteousness, sins, faithfulness, and weaknesses. God still knew it and left it up to Jeremiah to stand and fight for his salvation.

We need to be incredibly careful when using an issue as a clarion call to the Christian faith as a call to arms for a political movement stoked by duplicitous characters; in that call are the makings of sectarianism.

Sectarian violence divides faiths, people, and countries, and once it starts, it is tough to stop.

Rosner brings a new twist to the question of identity and, more importantly, "Biblical Identity." "One cannot ask who I am without first asking what I am. And to whom do I belong?" (Rosner, 2017)[3] These three interrelated questions allow us to delve much deeper into personal identity as it relates legally to citizenship, census status, and voting rights.

We are now six months into President Trump's second term as the President of the United States. And as he has promised, we are witnessing mass deportations across the country, ICE officers carrying out many clandestine raids throughout the country. The rule of law is disobeyed, judges are publicly disparaged, law firms and universities are threatened with investigations, and funding and tax exemption status are revoked. In addition, we are witnessing unprecedented firings of

---

3   Brian S. Rosner, Known by God (Grand Rapid: Harper Collins, 2017), 36

federal workers and life-threatening cuts to critical social funding programs. Thus far, the Hispanic communities have borne the brunt of the deportation activities, which shows a racial intention to this program; most believe that it will not end with this community. The first six months of this administration have shown extraordinarily little Christian virtue, despite proclaiming that we should live by the Christian faith. They fail to display God's love for the foreigner, his compassion for the poor, and his mercy for the sinner. This deportation by ethnicity looks more like a racial profiling program than a criminal finding one. And programs like these, which are done so blatantly and proudly, never make a country or the society of that country look great.

Chapter 3

RELIGIOUS OR IMPERIALISTIC CONFLICTS

Exodus 3: 7-8

And the Lord said, "I have indeed seen the oppression of My people who are in Egypt and have heard their cry because of their taskmasters, for I know their sorrows. So, I have come down to deliver them out of the hand of the Egyptians, and to bring them up from that land to a good and large land, to a land flowing with milk and honey, to the place of the Canaanites and the Hittites and the Amorites and the Perizzites and the Hivites and the Jebusites.

Politics leveraging the power of religious belief is not a new phenomenon. Long before the colonization of the Americas, this trend has been repeated throughout recorded history. Perhaps no area is more infamous for religious and imperialistic conflicts than the Middle East…

Israel's Assimilation

Before the assimilation timeline, Israel, also known as the Hebrews, was a collective unit of twelve nomadic tribes wandering in the wilderness until God gave them a large territory to inhabit. Moses, the Hebrew deliverer, brought his people out of Egyptian bondage in the 13th century BCE. After wandering in the wilderness for forty years, they entered Canaan in 1250 BCE from the southwest side of the Dead Sea near Bethel and Shechem, now present day "The West Bank. The present-day Palestinian argument against Israeli occupation is that this was an imperialistic act done through war and aggression, and not God.

After finally getting complete control over the land with King David's complete victory over the Philistines, Israel lived as a united nation from 1000 BCE until the Assyrian deportation began in 731 BCE. This 269-year period of unity is deceptive because King Solomon died in 931 BCE, 69 years after his father united the kingdom. Hence, the Israelites lived in a fully unified kingdom for 69 years, followed by a divided kingdom marked by cessions, strife, fighting, political upheaval, assassinations, and corruption for 200 years, until the northern kingdom was removed. The biblical books of Chronicles and Kings provide a comprehensive account of history and timelines.

Judah's Captivity

After Assyria assimilated and deported the Northern Kingdom from 731 to 722 BCE, only the Southern Kingdom of Judah and Benjamin remained. However, the Babylonian Empire under King Nebuchadnezzar initiated deportation proceedings in 605 BCE, with a return date of 536 BCE. This completed the seventy-year exile prophecy spoken about in Jeremiah 29:10.

Even after the three waves of returning refugees, Israel did not regain complete independence for another four hundred years at the end of the Maccabean Revolt. Then it was quickly occupied again, this time by the Roman Empire. Throughout Israel's entire existence, the one constant has been occupation by foreign invaders. These occupations were imperialistic because each invasion benefited the invaders by acquiring resources, including taxes, grain, oil, labor, and strategic military positions.

Occupation

Throughout Israel's history, they have had the distinguished pleasure of being conquered, occupied, and ruled by foreign sovereign nations seven times. So, while we can never forgive the recent events in the Gaza Strip, we can understand their mindset.

In 722 BCE, the Assyrians deported approximately

27,290 people over a period of eleven years. Due to the vast size of the Assyrian Empire (approximately 540,543 sq miles), the deportees were relocated from Israel eastward, approximately 500 to 600 miles, to Upper Mesopotamia, which is currently on the borders of Syria, Iraq, and Iran.

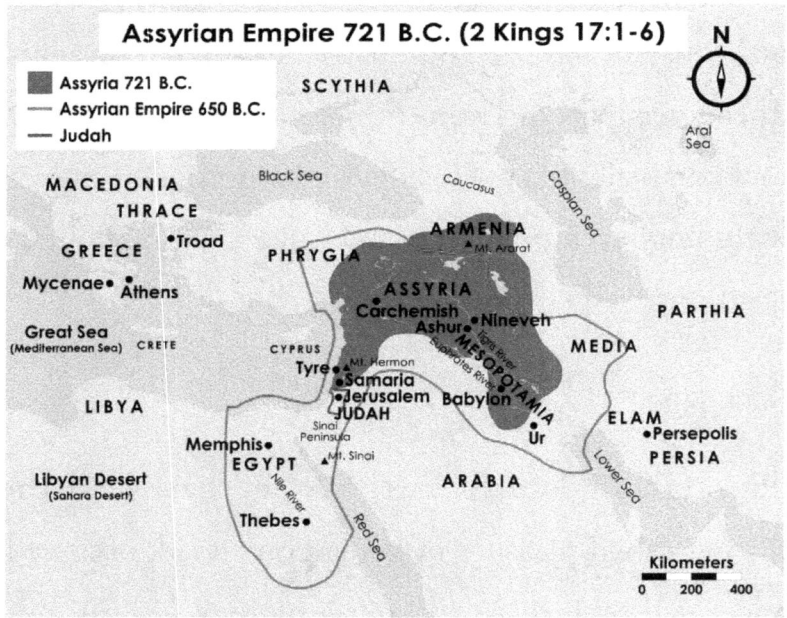

The Babylonian deportations began circa 605 BCE. The Babylonian Empire was significantly smaller than the Assyrian Empire, approximately 193,050

square miles. However, the deportation journey was much longer (at least 900 miles). Babylon was located directly east of Judah, where the northern tribes were located in Lebanon, and extended northeast to Upper Mesopotamia.

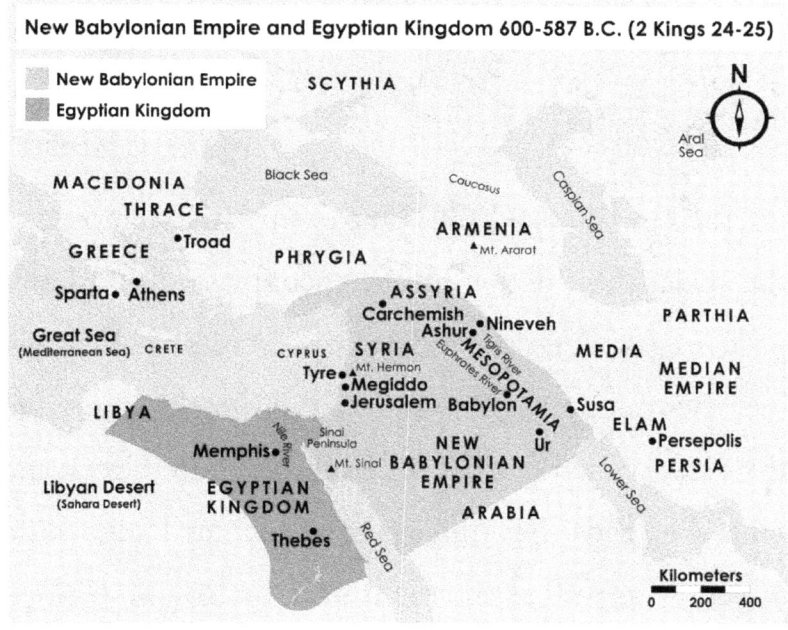

The Persians, 539 BCE: This empire fulfilled biblical prophecy when King Cyrus began returning the Israelites to Israel, even though many Babylonian Jews who were born in Babylon chose to remain.

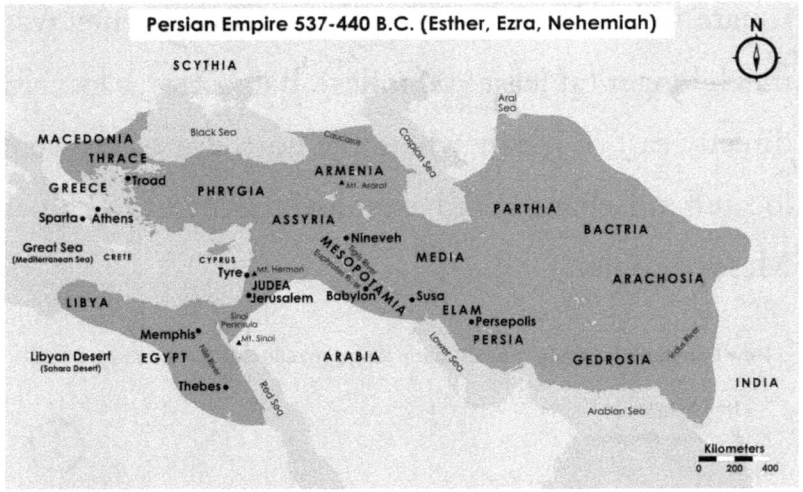

The Greeks, 490 BCE: One of the largest empires of the ancient world, this empire encompassed significant parts of Asia, Africa, and Europe. At its peak, it was over two million square miles. The Greeks translated the Hebrew text of the Old Testament into Greek and built the roads that missionaries, such as Paul, would travel on, as well as the roads used by Roman legions.

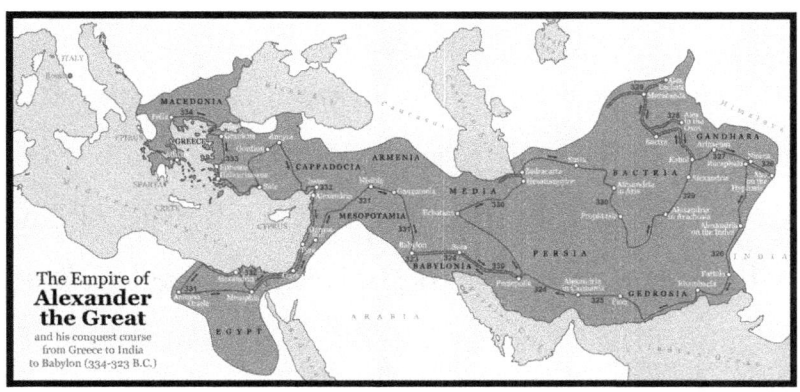

The Empire of **Alexander the Great** and his conquest course from Greece to India to Babylon (334-323 B.C.)

The Romans, 146 BCE: While much more extensive in population and landmass than the Greek empire, it is not the largest empire in history. That belongs to the British Empire. The Romans subjugated Israel while eventually setting Christianity free to become the official religion of the empire.

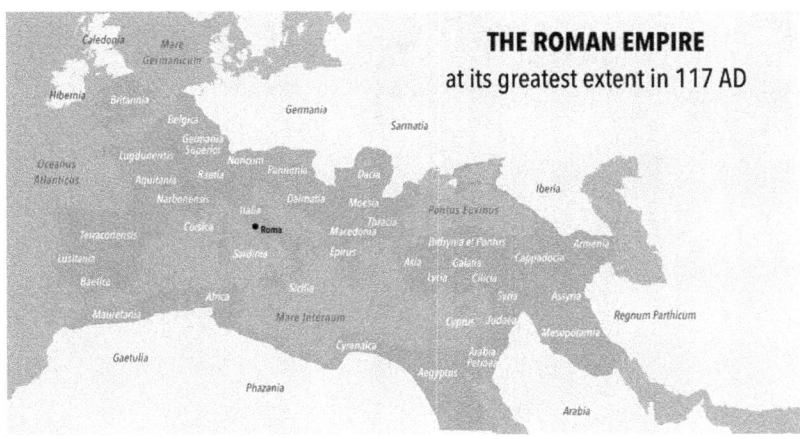

Crusades

The Crusades were a series of eight campaigns, often referred to as "Holy Wars," between the Islamic and Christian faiths over control of a small piece of land called Jerusalem and the holy sites sacred to both religions. The Crusades lasted from 1096 to 1300 CE.

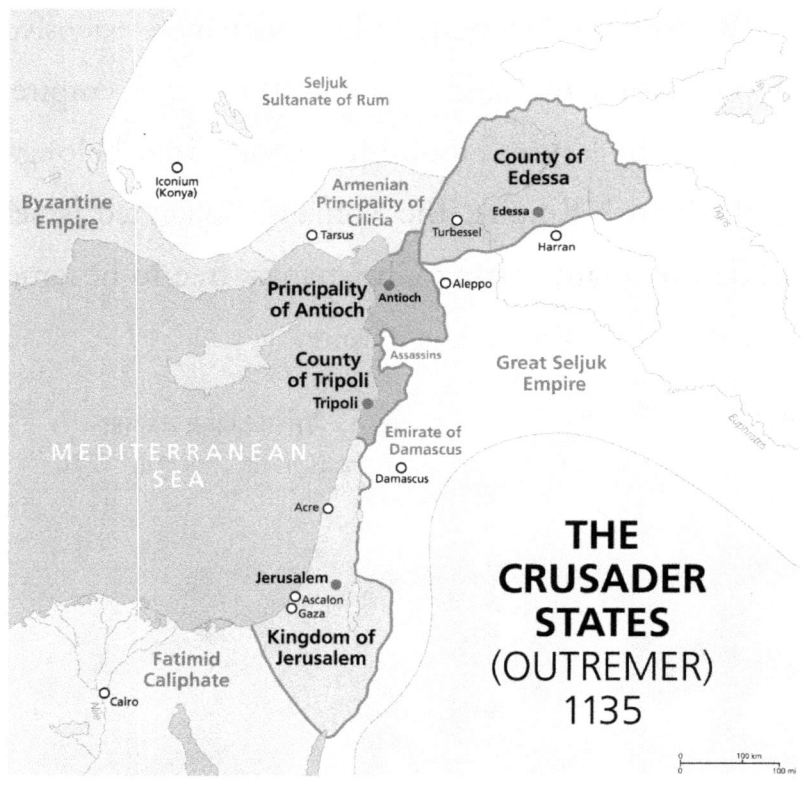

After the Muslim empire had captured Jerusalem, they could follow Muhammad's instructions to observe "Qibla" by facing Jerusalem during daily prayers. Pope Urban 2 then, in 1092, called for a crusade to retake and liberate Christian sites under Muslim control in the Holy Land, but more importantly, to stop the emerging Muslim power in the region. On the surface, the decree presented by the "Council of Clermont" was portrayed as a battle for God. Still, it was motivated by an imperialistic agenda to control Jerusalem and the surrounding region.

Historians estimate that the conflict lasted from 196 to 205 years, claiming between 1 and 3 million lives. In addition to battlefield deaths, lives were lost to starvation, disease, and revenge killings and murders by criminals. The Crusades ushered in a new kind of modern warfare, making European countries more open to imperialistic behaviors.

The Ottoman Empire

It is regarded as one of the world's longest-running empires. Officially, it ruled from 1299 to 1922, a total of 623 years. The Ottoman Empire was a multi-religious, multi-racial, multi-ethnic empire with a well-tuned military and an imperialistic mission led by one imperial sultan. It controlled a land mass of over two million square miles at its peak. Due to the empire's vastness, the Ottomans established the Millet System. A system in which each minority religious group was allowed to self-govern and be led by one spiritual leader who reported directly to the Ottoman Sultan.

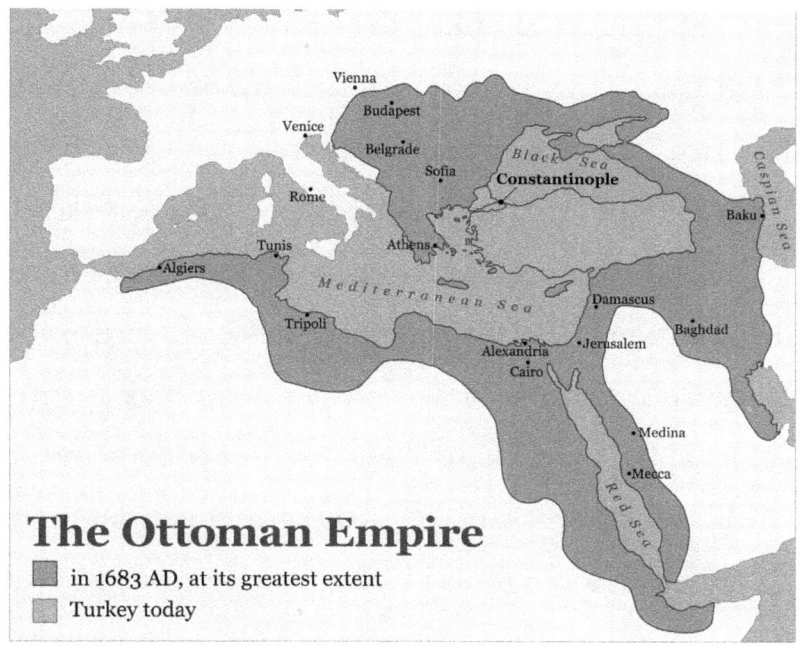

The Ottoman Empire
■ in 1683 AD, at its greatest extent
■ Turkey today

This last occupation set the stage for the state of Israel we see today. Following the Ottoman Empire's defeat at the end of World War I, British Foreign Secretary Arthur James Balfour proposed establishing a Jewish homeland in Palestine. At the end of World War I, following the defeat of Germany and the Ottoman Empire, the Balfour Declaration was applied to Palestine and approved by the League of Nations in 1922. This declaration dismantled the Ottoman Empire and granted Britain complete oversight of Palestine and Arab lands. This lasted until the end of World War II, when Israel became an independent state in 1948.

The 1949 Armistice Agreement between Israel, Lebanon, Syria, Jordan, and Egypt drew clear demarcation lines between Israel and Arab territories. Because Israel has never officially abided by this agreement, it has led to Israeli/Arab conflicts in the Middle East ever since. All these occupations were shrouded in a religious cloak but were driven by an imperialistic agenda, particularly evident in the Crusades and the Ottoman Empire.

CHAPTER 4

THE THOUGHTS OF MAN

Genesis 6:3

And the Lord said, 'My Spirit shall not strive with man forever, for he is indeed flesh; yet his days shall be one hundred and twenty years.'

In God's assessment of the entirety and totality of man's existence, he concluded that his spirit or ways would never eternally align with man's spirit due to the proclivities and propensities of man's dual nature. That man could never commit to a spiritual and selfless lifestyle eternally, so his lifespan would be shortened.

Magna Carta

The Magna Carta, written in the twelfth century (1215), was the first document to show man's dual nature at war with itself. The document established that no man, not even kings, was above the law. It was written by barons and landowners of the time to protect their property from the oppressive nature of kings. It established limited individual rights among the wealthy and the ruling class while limiting the king's absolute power.

The Magna Carta sought to limit the tyrannical whims of kings over barons and landowners, who limited the authoritarian whims of barons and landowners over the poor and indentured. While England was creating a more balanced and just society for itself and its aristocracy, simultaneously, they were becoming one of the worst imperialistic colonial superpowers the world has ever witnessed.

At the height of the British Empire's power, they were the largest empire in the history of the world. They controlled over 420 million people and were the world's leading power for a century, accounting for 23% of the world's population. The key to their power was exploiting goods from their colonies for trade and use in England. At one point, they were the number one player in the transatlantic slave trade. Transporting slaves from their colonies in Africa to their colonies in the West Indies.

The duality of this government to enshrine into law a more perfect and just society for themselves while simultaneously practicing the most brutal forms of imperialism, racism, and, in some cases, genocide brings a more explicit understanding to the scripture in Genesis 6:3.

The American Bill of Rights

The original founding document of the United States found its roots in England's Magna Carta. Its foundational principles are built on the selective granting of individual rights to specific segments of society. The document stipulates the rights of American citizens concerning their government, guaranteeing all American Citizens individual civil rights and liberties, including freedom of speech, freedom of the press, and freedom of religion. It also established due process under the law.

The United States of America was a former colony of the British Empire until it won its independence during the American Revolution. Penned the "American Bill of Rights" that was quickly drafted into the U.S Constitution, which has at its very opening statement and proclamation.

"We hold these truths to be self-evident, that all men are created equal; that their Creator endows them with certain unalienable rights; that among these are

Life, Liberty, and the pursuit of Happiness; that, to secure these rights, governments are instituted among Men, deriving their just powers from the consent of the governed; that whenever any form of government becomes destructive of these ends, it is the right of the people to alter or to abolish it, and to institute new government, laying its foundation on such principles, and organizing its powers in such form, as to them shall seem most likely to affect their safety and happiness. Prudence, indeed, will dictate that long-established governments should not be changed for light and transient causes, and accordingly, all experience hath shown that mankind is more disposed to suffer. At the same time, evils are sufferable than to right themselves by abolishing the forms to which they are accustomed. But when a long train of abuses and usurpations, pursuing invariably the same object, evinces a design to reduce them under absolute despotism, it is their right, it is their duty, to throw off such government and to provide new guards for their future security."

This proclamation was written to protect all American citizens except the slaves who had been here longer than most, worked harder than most, earned less than most, and suffered more than most. Once again, the duality and partiality in man's nature to disperse charity and suffering from the same basket puts him at odds with his God.

The Constitution of the Fifth Republic

This founding document of France was born out of a crisis and war, with some even suggesting a civil war. The Algiers crisis in 1958 highlighted the instability of the "French Fourth Republic." France, a colonial power at the time, struggled with the cries for separation from its colonies, including French West Africa, French Indochina, and French Algeria. On the advice of Charles de Gaulle, the government of the Fourth Republic voted to dissolve itself and form a new government, known as the Constitution of the Fifth Republic. In October 1958, the new and current constitution was adopted and has been amended (58) times to date. Some key features of the French constitution are:

- The parliament elects the President to a five-year term with one renewable term
- The president has more power than the parliament
- It has built-in core principles like:
  - Separation of church and state
  - Social welfare system
  - Indivisibility of rights that cannot be separated from their citizens

France, like England, displayed gross duplicities in promoting the motherland and the indivisibility of its laws and civil rights toward its citizens, as compared to how it treated its colonial possessions. They were a massive colonial power that exploited the resources and labor of colonized people in the Americas, Africa, Asia, and the Pacific Islands. They were the most brutal of the superpowers in their desire to promote French civilization, culture, and politics. They took diverse resources like cotton, tobacco, gold, and diamonds, and like Britain and Spain, the labor force of the empire was made up of black Africans taken from the African countries, as they were heavily involved in the slave trade.

The Behavior of Man

These are a few examples of men's words as they pertain to their vision for the fair governance of their fellow man. These documents are imperfect and have evolved over many years, during which men committed atrocities against one another. As explicitly stated in the Epistle of James 2:1-3, ***"My brethren, do not hold the faith of our Lord Jesus Christ, the Lord of glory, with partiality. Suppose there should come into your assembly a man with gold rings in fine apparel, and there should also come in a poor man in filthy clothes. In that case, you pay attention to the one wearing the fine clothes and say to him, 'You sit here in a good place,' and say to the poor man, 'You stand*** *there,' or, 'Sit here at my footstool,' have you not shown partiality among yourselves, and become judges with evil thoughts?"*

Our inability to trust God with our deepest desires and our ongoing desire to judge, condemn, and persecute others we feel are less worthy than us while puffing ourselves up in virtuous manners and speaking, competing, comparing, and performing within the faith have made many potential disciples run away from us, embarrass the Holy Church, and shame God's name among his created people.

Matthew 16:4, *"A wicked and adulterous generation seeks after a sign, and no signs shall be given to them, except the sign of the prophet Jonas. And he left them and departed."*

The arrogance of believers today rivals that of the Pharisees, who sought signs of their choosing while ignoring the signs that relieved the poor and the sick.

Daniel 7:2-7, *"Daniel spoke, saying, 'I saw in my vision by night, and behold, the four winds of heaven were* *stirring up the Great Sea. And four great beasts came up from the sea, each different from the other. The first was like a lion and had an eagle's wings. I watched till its wings were plucked off, lifted from the earth, and made to stand on two feet like a man, and a man's heart was given to it. And suddenly another beast, a second, like a bear. It was raised on one side and had three ribs in its mouth between its teeth. And they said thus to it: 'Arise, devour much flesh!' After this, I looked, and there was another, like a leopard with four wings on its back, like a bird. The beast also had four heads, and dominion was given to it. After this, I saw in the night visions, and behold, a fourth beast, dreadful, exceedingly strong. It had huge iron teeth, devouring, breaking in pieces, and trampling the residue with its feet. It was different from all the beasts before it and had ten horns.'"*

Daniel's prophetic vision disturbed his spirit about the four dominant world powers to come and how God sees man's imperialistic and war-minded behaviors. What shocked him so much was the indescribable fourth beast and its descendants, who would dominate and destroy the entire world.

England and France are direct descendants of this beast, having been conquered by it and adopting its form of government and behavior. The United States is an indirect descendant, as it was colonized by both France and England and adopted its forms of government and behaviors. These societies continue to be guided by their founding principles, which consistently exhibit a duality in their beliefs and behaviors.

The challenge for these societies is the commitment required to maintain and sustain the real-life and real-time applications of the progressive benefits of their founding principles for all citizens. This has always been an elusive task due primarily to the sinful nature of human beings, who are the dominant race and culture of said society and country. Until humans can overcome their struggles with racism, culturalism, tribalism, sexism, and ageism, they will always lead with their duality, saying one thing while meaning another.

CHAPTER 5

THE DESIRES OF MAN

Proverbs 27:20

Hell, and Destruction are never complete;
So, the eyes of man are never satisfied.

God's word speaks about the insatiable appetite of man's desire; as hell is never complete, man's desires are never satisfied. And if no discipline is attached to one's desires, they become uncontrollable. Discipline must be connected to our desires because of their consuming potency. But desire also runs deep and can connect to our characters forever.

Almost all human conflict stems from people pursuing their desires without discipline. The disputes can range from mundane and insignificant to life-threatening and terrifying. The self-destructive desire also prompts a person to engage in destructive behavior in an attempt to fulfill it. Let's paint a picture and show some examples of what this looks like.

Desire Without Discipline

Human beings are born with desire, a potent motivating emotion. Officially, desire is a strong feeling of wanting or wishing something to happen. This ebb and flow between wanting and wishing is where desire and its potency can become extremely dangerous to our lives and the lives of others who are perceived as threats to our desired objects or people. In a previous chapter, I used the scripture below to describe how our sinful desires can be so dangerous as to blind us to our new life and way of thinking and perceiving.

James 1:13-14, *"But each one is tempted when he is drawn away by his desires and enticed. Then, when desire has conceived, it gives birth to sin; when it is full-grown, sin brings forth death."*

When people become consumed by desire, they lose control of their rational decision-making skills and are led down a destructive path of unrighteousness, lust, and violent behaviors. This can happen professionally as one seeks and craves a higher position with a more significant title, recognizable status, and increased income. The signs of this are loosening one's moral compass, as evidenced by dehumanizing or dismissive behavior, and the perception of a perceived threat.

The Highjacking of a Faith

It can begin with character assassination, slander, and outright lies. It can escalate into recruiting others in this unrighteous behavior.

Many of us lose our way through a desire to do good, as in the case of Jim Jones, the pastor of the "Peoples Temple," who desired to create a new theology called "Apostolic Socialism" and incorporate it into communal lifestyles for the congregation. Due to local opposition from the municipality, he believed he would have better control over the congregation outside of the laws of the United States. In trying to build this Christian Kibbutz of shared life, his desires and misperceived threats led him down a very dark path that ultimately led to the murder of over nine hundred people, which included two hundred children.

David Koresh, the cult leader of the Branch Davidians, strongly desired to be the final prophet and a type of the Messiah. His apocalyptic vision of faith and the world led him to isolate himself and his followers in a Waco, Texas, compound and engage in armed combat with the US government law enforcement agencies. Koresh and his followers set their compound on fire, killing seventy-nine followers.

People with passionate desires without discipline can be hazardous to themselves and those around them. The two men that I mentioned did not wake up and decide to become mass murderers of the people they professed to love the most, nor did they believe they would ever violate their faith and obedience to the word of God so wholly and highly. Yet their desires became runaway trains, dragging them and many others to disastrous ends.

Human desire is almost always self-centered, selfish, and passionate. When fulfilled, it can give us euphoria and a false sense of security. It has a voracious appetite and must be fed constantly. In these circumstances, we often overlook the natural obstacles to fulfillment and instead focus on misperceived ones. This is because our desires are intricately connected to our egos, which fuel our narcissism to be correct at any cost.

When King David stood on his balcony on that clear night and saw the natural physical beauty of Bathsheba, his ongoing struggles with lustful desire got the best of him, which led him to a series of irrational and deadly decisions that cost him his kingship, an innocent man his life, the death of his son and disbarment from building God's Holy Temple. Eve's desire to receive knowledge from the Tree of Good and Evil cost humanity residency in the Garden of Eden, and Cain's desire to be recognized by God over his brother led to the first murder in human history.

There are many kinds of unrestrained desire, but the following are some of the more common pitfalls.

Sexual Lust

Often disguised as love, the Bible identifies this as "Eros" love and limits its practice only to marriage. It is viewed as a self-satisfying, selfish type of love. People who have an out-of-control lust desire often struggle with fidelity and selflessness. This desire acts immediately on what it sees as pleasing to the eye. One of the most famous examples is the previously mentioned encounter between King David and Bathsheba.

2 Samuel 11:2-4, *"Then it happened one evening that David arose from his bed and walked on the roof of the king's house. From the roof, he saw a woman bathing, and the woman was beautiful. So, David sent an inquiry about the woman. And someone said, 'Is this Bathsheba, the daughter of Eliam, the wife of Uriah the Hittite?' Then David sent messengers and took her, and she came to him, and he lay with her, for she was cleansed from her impurity, and she returned to her house."*

This one simple act of giving in to lustful desire brought about many devastating and deadly ends. Uriah, the Hittite, who was Bathsheba's husband, was killed, as was Absalom, David's son. David lost his throne, and even his daughter was raped by her brother.

Many famous people fall victim to this love. Tiger Woods claimed to have been diagnosed with a sexual addiction after being caught cheating on his wife and allegedly linked to thirteen women who came forth to say they had had encounters with him. In this case, the desire became so intense by constantly feeding it that it manifested into a physical and psychological addiction.

The Hollywood movie producer Harvey Weinstein, unlike Tiger Woods, fed his lustful desires through the power and manipulation of the vulnerable. His lust was so intense that he was convicted of raping and blackmailing his victims.

Love of Money

In today's world, money represents power, financial security, exclusivity, and entitlement. A desire for these things consumes most people who are driven by a love of money. Life outside of these things consists of the daily routine of the nine-to-five grind, where you eke out a living with no power to control your autonomy, little financial security, and absolutely zero exclusivity in anything you do or anywhere you go. Facing these predicaments, most people consider expanding their financial footprint daily. A desire to avoid this type of life is highly consuming, and the easiest way to rise above it is by accumulating money.

All consumption begins with the desire to have. The avenues we choose to fulfill this desire will be determined by our dissatisfaction with our circumstances, as well as our level of maturity and morality. The more dissatisfied we become, the less moral and mature paths we will choose. The apostle Paul gives us an antidote to this consuming desire:

Philippians 4: 6-7, *"Do not be anxious about anything, but in every situation, by prayer and petition, with thanksgiving, present your requests to God. And the peace of God, which transcends all understanding, will guard your hearts and minds in Christ Jesus."*

Philippians 4:11-13, *"I am not saying this because I am in need, for I have learned to be content whatever the circumstances. I know what it's like to be in need and what it's like to have plenty. I have learned the secret of being content in any and every situation, whether well-*

fed or hungry, whether living in plenty or want. I can do all this through him who gives me strength."

Those who do not learn to be contented, satisfied, and grateful for what they have tend to live lives of extreme excess, often driven by a craving for entitlement. Professional athletes, corporate CEOs, and celebrities have all achieved the goal of accumulating enormous wealth only to display lives of excess and entitlement publicly. This behavior is the engine's core, which drives and motivates and must constantly be fed.

Love of Power

We have created a society where people's activities have become a significant part of their identities, especially in the professional and career realms. Most people, knowingly or unknowingly, identify themselves by what they do for a living. "I am a police officer, I am a pastor, I am a doctor." Sometimes, it is done by identifying with the affiliations or organizations to which they belong. "I am a Christian, a member of the Democratic or

Republican Parties." This is done to perpetuate these ongoing behaviors:

- Live life strategically and socialize only within those groups
- View meeting people as networking opportunities to get something
- Constantly maneuvering oneself to gain access to power
- Becoming duplicitous in speech

The desire for power is not a new phenomenon to humanity. At the fall of the "Garden of Eden," a power struggle was placed on humanity between the sexes. The first power struggle will be within us, a fight to control our consciousness through raw natural emotions or sound, rational, spirit-led thinking. The next will be between the sexes, man and woman. No longer are the days of harmony; there will be an ongoing fight to be unified and stay so because this fight is truly a hidden war, as I described in detail in my third book, "The Corporate Christian 3: The Hidden War."

Mark 7:20-23, *"And He said, "What comes out of a man, which defiles a man. For from within, out of the heart of men, proceed evil thoughts, adulteries, fornications, murders, thefts, covetousness, wickedness, deceit, lewdness, an evil eye, blasphemy, pride, foolishness. All these evil things come from within and defile a man."*

Genesis 3:15-16, *"And I will put enmity Between you and the woman, And between your seed and her Seed; He shall bruise your head, And you shall bruise His heel." To the woman, He said: "I will greatly multiply your sorrow and your conception; In pain, you shall bring forth children; Your desire shall be for your husband, And he shall rule over you."*

Proverbs 14:30-31, *"A sound heart is life to the body, but envy is rottenness to the bones. He who oppresses the poor reproaches his Maker, but he who honors Him has mercy on the needy.*

Society has gone so far off course that, through

our arrogance, we now even challenge God's wisdom. God speaks through the Apostle Paul in the Book of Romans to remind us that all authority comes from Him and that we must submit to His authority because His path for us is far better than any path we may devise. This can be an almost unbearable task for the power-hungry and control freaks among us, for their desire is never to submit to but have people submit to them and their whims, which are almost always self-gratifying to them by design.

Love of Status: Pride

The need to be recognized, praised, and adored, the desire for titles and entitlements, and the insatiable pursuit of not just being great but for all to know of your greatness can be wrapped up in one word: Pride. As some have said, it is the deadliest of sins and the gateway to all sin in our lives. It represents a crashing of morality in an individual and a cascading of other character defects coming to the surface. The following scripture lists it as the first sin in a list of seven that God considers a moral crisis in a person's heart:

Proverbs 6:16-19, *"These six things the L*ORD *hates, Yes, seven are an abomination to Him: A proud look, A lying tongue, Hands that shed innocent blood, A heart that devises wicked plans, Feet that are swift in running to evil, A false witness who speaks lies, And one who sows discord among brethren."* In summary, it reflects on someone who causes unnecessary strife among people as abominable. Psychologists will tell us that this type of unnecessary acting out stems from immaturity and underdeveloped coping skills from an individual's youth.

Certain professions are particularly susceptible to this sin: those that involve working with the public and require a positive public image, such as clergy, politicians, and entertainers. These professions attract immensely proud people. In these professions, character truly matters; it helps you stay grounded in God and His holy word.

Affluence Vs. Influence

Many societies, including the United States, measure the success of their population on several indicators.

- Wellness
- Health
- Mental Health
- Wealth

The first three are measured through health information and health records; these indicators are typically found in the Center for Medicare and Medicaid Services (CMS), the Centers for Disease Control and Prevention (CDC), and the National Institutes of Health (NIH). These federal agencies monitor the population's health through infection control, vaccine immunizations, and hospital record reviews, conducting audits and inspections to ensure compliance. They have never conducted a detailed study on the impact of wealth on the population's health and how the distribution of wealth in a capitalist society affects a population's overall health, either positively or negatively.

As a Christian pastor, I am reminded of the scripture in the 3rd Epistle of **John 1-4, *"The Elder, To the beloved Gaius, whom I love in truth: Beloved, I pray that you may prosper in all things and be healthy, just as your soul prospers. For I rejoiced greatly when brethren came and testified of the truth in you, just as you walk in the truth. I have no greater joy than to hear that my children walk in truth.***

The epistle reveals a symbiotic relationship between money and advocacy, affluence, and influence that should always be at the forefront of the nation's consciousness. This relationship cannot be outsourced to government agencies alone but should be a clarion call to all, reminding us that we are our brother's keepers. One of the ways Christ told us that we could fulfill the commandments was to "Love the Lord thy God with all our heart, with all our minds, and with all our souls and our neighbors likewise." In this, we begin to live by faith rather than sight and demonstrate the mustard seed kind of faith that removes the mountains that separate and divide us as a species.

In global human capitalistic societies, the desire to follow affluent and decadent lifestyles is strong, and the effects of its pull can be seen in the rich and poor alike: the rich, through the accumulation of assets and quality of life, and the poor, with their obsessions, dreams, desires, and quality of life. As I stated earlier, having financial wealth provides a person with economic security, excess, exclusivity, and entitlements to fulfill most of their desires. Scripture never speaks against acquiring riches; it is only about the love of it because in that love, one is led away from advocating for the poor through an entitled belief system. Wealthy trappings are presented to the world to entice all who would choose them over influential advocacy.

An influential advocate is someone who, through success and access, has the means and platform to speak out against unfair wealth distribution, corporate greed, tax equity, and the indifference shown toward the poor and working poor. Christ, with his disciples, looked at the rich and affluent bringing offerings into the temple. They were giving large amounts of money, but in the midst of them, an old woman walked in and gave two cents, and Christ commented that out of all of them, she had given the most because they had given out of their abundance, whereas she had given out of her poverty, she had given all she had.

The message here is not to hoard wealth; use it to make accurate and instantaneous impacts in the lives of real people. This type of charity emerges when we resist affluence and its promises of extraordinary and exciting lives through travel, abundance, and excess.

CHAPTER 6

THE RULES OF MAN

Galatians 3:28

There is neither Jew nor Greek nor slave nor free;
there is neither male nor female,
for you are all one in Christ Jesus.

Putting one type or class of person above another and elevating those select few into roles of leadership and privilege is an example of elitism. We can observe numerous examples of this in American society, particularly regarding race, wealth, social status, or gender.

Dangers of Elitism

One of the most easily visible examples of elitism in American politics is the putting of men above women. With the presidential election loss of Vice President Harris to Former President Trump, the questions must be: Is America a male-dominated society? And if so, what does this look like?

Historically, America has always been a male-dominated society, but great strides have been made over the last one hundred and twenty years to achieve gender equality. But with the recent events of the overturning of Roe Vs Wade, the avalanche of States passing draconian laws to restrict reproductive rights, and the criminalizing of medical facilities, abortion clinics, and organizations like Planned Parenthood, the country is moving back in a direction to solidify its patriarchal identity. This identity was initially perverted in 1620 England by a political theorist named Sir Robert Filmer. He believed in the absolute power of the king and male dominance.

With this identity comes rules of being and existing in this old and, in some cases, new reality. This new reality still reveals inconsistencies between human behavior and God's requirements for social living and interaction standards. Here are a few of God's requirements for men:

Ephesians 5:25-28, *"Husbands love your wives, as Christ loved the church and gave himself up for her, that he might sanctify her, having cleansed her by the washing of water with the word, so that he might present the church to himself in splendor, without spot or wrinkle or any such thing, that she might be holy and without*

blemish. In the same way, husbands should love their wives as they love their bodies. He who loves his wife loves himself.

According to God, husbands are commanded to love their wives as they love their bodies. No one abuses, cheats, or steals from themselves; they do not disrespect or dominate themselves. It would be best to do it for your wife as you would for yourself, physically, emotionally, and spiritually.

God has given men a uniquely challenging role in the family. His responsibility in the family is to reflect that of Jesus Christ Himself. He is charged with nurturing and caring for every family member, with the same tenderness and loving authority Christ has for His Church. It is a role of honor and responsibility, not one of authority and domination.

The inconsistency between man's rules and God's requirements is vast and drastic. God requires men to be intense, tender, emotionally controlled, and intimate.

In other words, God includes balance in everything we do, think, believe, and behave to use as guardrails against the extreme sides of our nature.

When we begin to walk with God, there is an ongoing maturing process that should never be interrupted; some call these interruptions' backsliding." Here is an example of this process:

1 Corinthians 10:12-13, *"Therefore let him who thinks he stands take heed lest he fall. No temptation has overtaken you except such as is common to man; but God is faithful, who will not allow you to be tempted beyond what you are able, but with the temptation will also make the way of escape, that you may be able to bear it."*

Temptation and resistance are part of life. The verses before these give examples of the children of Israel and how they were overtaken by the temptations of idolatry, sexual immorality, and complaining amid their deliverance. Many Americans likewise find themselves gripped in the throngs of complaining, gripping, and mumbling about life; others wrestle with idol worship of jobs, money, and materialistic possessions, and yet others struggle with lust and sexual immorality. Therefore, we should always be mindful of our thoughts, desires, situations, and circumstances, as well as, most importantly, the presence of God and His way of helping us escape temptation.

Pride of Elitism

It has been said that pride is a foundational sin upon which all other sins are built. It was the first sin when Satan refused to recognize God as Lord and was removed from the Garden of God. Pride can be as hard as steel and almost impossible to bend, which makes it so dangerous to all of us.

Proverbs 16:18-19 says, *"Pride goes before destruction And a haughty spirit before a fall. It is better to be humble with the lowly than to divide the spoiled with the proud."*

This sin of pride always leads to the destruction of oneself and the innocent around one. Prideful leaders prioritize their desires over the people they lead;

similarly, prideful CEOs prioritize their pride over their companies, often at the expense of their employees' livelihoods. King David's pride put the Davidic covenant in jeopardy over prideful lust; how many leaders have allowed their prideful sexual lust to terrorize the opposite sex at work, leading to sexual harassment investigations? How many workers have been wrongfully terminated due to prideful leaders, resulting in costly litigation and negative publicity? It is much better and more peaceful to be humble and walk with the lowly than to enjoy the depraved spoils of pride. And here lies the center of the problem:

Proverbs 18:11-12, *"The rich man's wealth is his strong city And like a high wall in his esteem. Before destruction, the heart of a man is haughty, and before honor is humility."*

Pride is singular-minded and blinding, so destruction is never seen; pride also gives a false sense of security and esteem. Most of us are already too deep to avoid destruction when destruction is within sight. The pride of elitism allows the ruling elite to explore many forbidden taboos through access and entitlement and the partaking of many sins.

Sins of Elitism

Pride can be a foundational sin in a person's life; Catholicism sees it as one of the seven deadliest sins, even more so for those with unfettered authority to indulge. Its symptoms are displayed within those who have an excessive love of self or their abilities. It controls individuals through vainglory and a strong desire to be loved or recognized. These individuals are bombarded daily with any of the following as tools to attract the attention they seek.

- Greed
- Corruption
- Lust
- Anger
- Covetousness

- Lying
- Gossip
- False Witness

Lust and anger are the two most common and deadly of these; they lead people to many consequences. The vainglory of pride blinds individuals with an excessive love of self and abilities, so they seek love, recognition, and/or lust from others. When they pursue love in a relationship, lust is right beside it. When they are rejected, anger is right there.

CHAPTER 7
THE ALLURE OF ATTENTION

Proverbs 16:18

Pride goes before destruction,
And a haughty spirit before a fall.

As the spread of information (both genuine and false) speeds up in the modern age, so does our desire for gratification. And little is more gratifying than seeing the instant reactions of others to our news, updates, photos, and creations. But God asks us to seek validation from Him, not the sin of self-worship.

The temptation behind these levels of attention can be strong, and like many of our human desires, if they are not tempered with discipline, they can consume us before we even become aware of them. At the extreme are those who seek attention to further their gains (political, business, or otherwise), no matter the cost. All it takes is for the average person to spread their negativity, often with ruinous results.

Attention Seekers at Pandemic Levels

The rise of the new industry, social media, and its conglomerates, such as Meta (Facebook), Instagram, Tik Tok, and Twitter (now known as X), has transformed how people obtain information, stay connected, sell their products, promote their brands, and express opinions across social media platforms. It has allowed the individual to be heard and the small and weak to speak and challenge the large and powerful.

At the same time, it has increased narcissistic entitlements and ushered in, at pandemic levels, a generation of "Attention Seekers." In their pursuit of attention, people sometimes consume the most debased, profane, outlandish, inaccurate, and even outright lies that dominate these spaces. These attention seekers, armed with these platforms, will now share it with their groups and continue to spread it, hoping for the attention it may or may not bring.

2 Timothy 4: 3-4, *"For the time will come when people will not put up with sound doctrine. Instead, they will gather many teachers around them to suit their desires and hear what their itching ears want. They will turn their ears away from the truth and turn aside to myths."*

The attention seekers are duplicitous in their motivations and deceitful in their character, for what they present is never who they are, and what they accept is never what they truly desire. This new phenomenon has caused a rift and division among the current generation because of a lack of trust, commitment, and sincerity.

As the country braces itself for a second Trump presidency, many women and minorities feel terrified and betrayed. The African American community believes that the White community voted against their economic interest to satisfy their racial interest, women think that men choose misogynistic interests over their own financial and freedom interests, and Hispanics voted to uphold colonial traditions and not support a person they see as a competitor because her skin was not white. These long-standing issues of race, power, and jealousy have added to the rift and division so that it has fragmented American society, even in our relationships.

Marriage and birth rates are declining at alarming rates, which is a contributing factor to this decline. According to the CDC, "The provisional number of births for the United States in 2023 was 3,591,328, down

2% from the number in 2022 (3,667,758). The number of births declined by an average of 2% per year from 2015 to 2020, including a decline of 4% from 2019 to 2020. However, it rose 1% from 2020 to 2021, likely due to the COVID-19 lockdown, and remained unchanged from 2021 to 2022 (3.8%). The provisional number of births declined 5% for American Indian and Alaska Native women, 4% for Black women, 3% for White women, and 2% for Asian women from 2022 to 2023. Births rose 1% for Hispanic women and remained unchanged for Native Hawaiian or Other Pacific Islander women." Many believe this is the real reason for a national abortion ban.

However, this phenomenon has not only affected the current generation; it has also dominated marketing philosophies and strategies. Both for-profit and nonprofit businesses are consuming it at pandemic levels, as it has been presented as the best way to increase the bottom line. As accurate as this marketing concept is, one should always look past the silver and gold to accurately evaluate the actual cost and who will collect the owed debt.

An example of this business quagmire is political campaigns; candidates hold rallies nationwide during national elections, stopping in many local municipalities and small towns, incurring significant expenses for these venues. These costs include overtime for police and fire departments, EMS, traffic control, and sanitation cleanup. Since 1992, with the Bill Clinton campaign, and up to the 2024 election season, national campaigns have struggled to reimburse these municipalities. And most never get reimbursement. The attitude of these campaigns seems to be that the areas that get to host a presidential campaign visit should be grateful because these visits generate so much publicity and increased spending due to an immediate increase in the population coming in for the campaign stop, hotel reservations, restaurant, and bar spending, airport and tolls fees all benefit the area. The problem with this accounting is that money is not an immediate reimbursement to cover the immediate overtime labor cost that will be incurred.

So, while social media marketing may attract attention for you and your business, it may not immediately increase your bottom line and, in many cases, may put you in the poor house.

Another dangerous precedent of tying attention-seeking to financial rewards is the newly emerging influencer marketing industry. This industry is based on the number of people an individual can attract as followers on their platform. In most cases, the collection methodology is salacious and lascivious, bordering on profane and debased behaviors. In promoting these platforms, individuals build their following and then use this base to negotiate deals with companies to hire them to sell their products to their followers. This self-serving industry is not concerned with morality or loyalty to its followers, the imagery it presents to them, or the quality of the products it is paid to sell. Their immediate desires for attention and money are being fulfilled, and that is all that matters.

The Transmittance

Unlike in Hollywood movies, where evil is depicted as being transferred by evil spirits entering humans through spiritual forms and then taking control of a person's mental and physical bodies to commit wicked acts, the transmission of evil and negativity in the world today is much more sinister, clinical, and subtle.

All infectious diseases are transmitted through one of two ways: waterborne or airborne. Spiritual wickedness is transmitted through audio wavelengths. Scripture teaches us in **Romans 10:17, *"So then faith comes by hearing, and hearing by the word of God."*** So, if faith comes by hearing god's word, fear, confusion, and discouragement come by hearing Satan's. The more negativity one consumes, the more corrupt one's heart becomes, and the darker one's vision becomes.

Scripture implores us to in **Philippians 4: 8**, *"Finally, brethren, whatever things are true, whatever things are noble, whatever things are just, whatever things are pure, whatever things are lovely, whatever things are of good report, if there is any virtue and if there is anything praiseworthy meditate on these things."*

And before this, it says in **Philippians 4:6**, *"Be anxious for nothing, but in everything by prayer and supplication, with thanksgiving, let your requests be made known to God; and the peace of God, which surpasses all understanding, will guard your hearts and minds through Christ Jesus."*

American society has become consumed with regurgitating rebellious, judgmental, accusatory, and defamatory information that it has heard from one platform or another and from one person who has heard it from another platform. This information is then shared via phone texts or social media posts with the general population for further consumption. The spread and consumption of this sinful behavior have spread faster than any known biological virus.

The only difference between sin and a virus is that sin comes more naturally to us and feels good when consumed. Satan dominates this world and blinds us so entirely that we fail to recognize this process even when it is right before our eyes.

Political Instigators

During the United States 2024 presidential elections, the Republican Party unleashed such an egregious lie that it was almost laughable until it was no longer, because that lie was then transmitted and spread through social media and instant messaging by attention-seekers and instigators, reaching millions.

The lie itself was directed toward the city of Springfield, Ohio, and its Haitian community, claiming that this community was eating the pets of its neighbors. President Trump made this claim on a national debate stage against Vice President Harris, with an audience of

67 million viewers watching. This hateful lie became a political instigation movement for the general population who shared these views with the Republican Party.

What followed was a series of events that threatened the lives of this community, its children, and its citizens. It was far-reaching, from the very tangible and daily bomb threats of schools, city buildings, grocery stores, houses of worship, and public spaces. The danger, chaos, and expense of constantly evacuating these places because President Trump put a target on the town via hate speech. The fear caused emotional toll on the children who were teased at school, while the parents are living in fear because of the mass deportation promises to come, even though they currently have temporary protected status.

It's essential to recognize that most politicians involved likely didn't care about anyone's pets and were aware that this was a gross misrepresentation of the truth. Still, it gave them a manufactured enemy to rally against and win an election.

Here, we see at least four of the six things the Lord hates wrapped up into one lie; this lie was so egregious that PolitiFact, a fact-checking political news group, named it " Lie of the Year." A lying tongue, a person who stirs up conflict in the community, a heart that devises wicked plans, a lying witness who testifies falsely.

This did not happen in 1930s Germany or 1990s Rwanda; it happened in North America, a country that prides itself on decency and respect for the rule of law. However, most of the Republican Party either believed this lie or were willing not to say anything against it. This is how the Holocaust, and the Rwandan genocide were allowed to happen; so-called good people turned a blind eye to it.

Radicalization

The spread of hate speech can have much further implications. Throughout the 1980s and up to and including the 911 terrorist attacks, we witnessed young men in the Islamic faith and White Christian nationalist movements begin to ingest an abnormal amount of hate speech and view sectarian and racist violence, which transformed their personalities. These young soldiers, for their movements, were controlled, pointed towards, and unleashed upon an innocent population to wreck and destroy property, kill and maim the innocent, and instill the maximum amount of fear.

Yet, we failed to recognize it for what it was and created new scientific terms to rationalize and understand it. Being complacent in the face of evil shows a lack of discernment and a failure to seek God's wisdom.

Proverbs 14:12 says, *"There is a way that seems right to a man, but its end is the way of death."* Romans 12:9 says, *"Let love be without hypocrisy. Abhor what is evil. Cling to what is good."*

CHAPTER 8

THE APPETITE OF HATE

Matthew 5: 43-44

You have heard that it was said, 'You shall love your neighbor and hate your enemy.' But I say to you, love your enemies, bless those who curse you, do good to those who hate you, and pray for those who spitefully use and persecute you.

The Highjacking of a Faith

Hate is a raw emotion that rarely operates in a vacuum but is always at the heart of complex societal issues played out among individuals. Many of these issues surround the competition for resources, quality of life standards, income disparity, racism, mass media propaganda, and peer pressure.

Throughout the 1930s, when Adolf Hitler and the Nazi party were on the rise in Germany, they manufactured an enemy for all Germans to hate. This goal was for the party to capture complete political control of the country and the minds of its citizens. Mass media propaganda systems were implemented to broadcast daily the superiority and purity of the Aryan race and the inferiority of everyone else, especially the Jewish citizens, whom they deemed as a financial threat to their power.

At the end of World War II, we saw the results of this campaign. The war ended with the saying, "Never Again," only to happen again. The 1994 Rwanda Civil War that led to the Rwanda genocide followed the same path as the Jewish Holocaust. An enemy was created for political gain; a society was indoctrinated and weaponized, and two months later, five hundred thousand Tutsis were slaughtered, murdered, raped, mutilated, and desecrated.

Stages of Hate

As stated, hate within itself is a powerful emotion, and God warns us not to indulge in it, even advising us not to let the sun go down with hate in our hearts because hate is a thing that can be transformed into a weapon of mass destruction.

Romans 12:20, *"If your enemy is hungry, feed him; if he is thirsty, give him a drink."*

Hate consumes in stages, from irritation to distancing, termination, and annihilation. These stages represent the consuming and downward direction that hate leads to. However, it does not take us there on its own, and this is where outside complexities play a significant part. The book of Proverbs, chapter 6, verse 16, begins with the writer telling us the six things the Lord hates. If we examine each one, they represent outside agitators who incite people against one another.

- A lying tongue: liars cause much confusion among people
- Hands that shed innocent blood: The sociopathic nature of hate
- Feet that are quick to rush into evil: The desire to participate in hatefulness
- A person who stirs up conflict in the community: The instigator
- Haughty eyes: The Narcissist
- A heart that devises wicked plans: The iniquity of hate
- A lying witness who testifies falsely: The betrayer

This insatiable appetite, with its strong desire to express hatred toward someone or something, reveals that hatred is not only present but is also actively consuming and growing, much like physical hunger for food.

Proverbs 10:12, *"Hatred stirs up strife, but love covers all offenses."*

Hatred is a fleeting emotion and a powerful force that drives someone's actions and thoughts. Like an uncontrolled appetite that can never be satisfied, the appetite for hate can lead to harmful behaviors and actions against its targets.

Combating Hate

Hate is a sin against God and others; the Christian is called to love God and his neighbor as himself. Hate is a heart issue; only God's love can replace it in the human heart. This begins with forgiving others and not harboring hatred for past offenses. This can't be accomplished without daily meditation on the word of God until revelation and understanding take hold of our minds and transform our thinking and behavior. Below are a few biblical scriptures that will help us in the battle; notice that they are written for us to act upon. No action on our part will lead to no victory in the fight.

Romans 12:19-20, *"Beloved, do not avenge yourselves, but rather give place to wrath; for it is written, 'Vengeance is Mine, I will repay,' says the Lord. Therefore, If your enemy is hungry, feed him; If he is thirsty, give him a drink; For in so doing you will heap coals of fire on his head."*

Matthew 5:22, *"But I say to you that whoever is angry with his brother without a cause shall be in danger of the judgment. And whoever says to his brother, 'Raca!' shall be in danger of the council. But whoever says, 'You fool!' shall be in danger of hellfire."*

Luke 6:27, *"But I say to you who hear: Love your enemies, do good to those who hate you."*

1 John 4:20, *"If someone says, 'I love God,' and hates his brother, he is a liar; for he who does not love his brother whom he has seen, how can he love God whom he has not seen?"*

These are just a few scriptures that God has given us to combat the hate in our hearts. These scriptures put the onus on us to be successful in this battle. This is an internal and personal battle, as was quoted: "Hatred is the poison we drink, hoping the other person will die" (Buddha). The only people hurt by hatred are those who hold and harbor it in their hearts.

A Demonic Design

Looking at the world today, you see the extensive division among people. Witnessing this phenomenon in action is incredible because it has helped resolve the division among people. The one thing all people seem to agree upon—Black people, White people, Asian people, Indian people, English people, French people, Scandinavian people, and Caribbean people—is that they dislike someone or their group and feel comfortable expressing their dislike in some form of public expression. Not even the gospel of love could unite the world so boldly in love and support for one another.

Where does this power of influence come from? Who can bring people who speak different languages, live in various geographies, and have different cultures to behave identically on one specific topic? I am talking about the power of evil and the one who wields it best, our great adversary Satan, the father of lies. Jesus Christ told us in the gospel of **John 10:10**, *"The thief does not come except to steal, and to kill, and to destroy. I have come that they may have life, and that they may have it more abundantly."*

Let us discuss killing, stealing, and destroying, and how these actions can turn us into walking zombies and a shell of our potential.

CHAPTER 9

STEPS OF A DEMONIC DESIGN

John 10:10

The thief does not come except to steal, and to kill, and to destroy. I have come that they may have life, and that they may have it more abundantly.

Now, before we get to Satan and his evil ways, we must first get to know Lucifer, the anointed shining star. God created a mighty, intelligent, and beautiful spirit and placed him over all angelic beings. His name was Lucifer, which meant "Shining One." He even had free choice, which he exercised incorrectly.

Isaiah 14: 12-14, *"How you have fallen from heaven, O Lucifer, son of the morning! How you are cut down to the ground, you who weakened the nations! For you have said in your heart: 'I will ascend into heaven, I will exalt my throne above the stars of God; I will also sit on the mount of the congregation On the farthest sides of the north; I will ascend above the heights of the clouds, I will be like the Most-High.'*

In these few scriptures, we see Lucifer defying God with his five I-will statements.

I will ascend into heaven

I will exalt my throne above the stars

I will also sit on the mount of the congregation

I will ascend above the heights

I will be like the Most High

A parallel description in the book of Ezekiel provides us with a little more insight into his fall and the reason behind it.

Ezekiel 28: 13-17, *"You were in Eden, the garden of God. I ordained and anointed you as the mighty angelic guardian. You had access to the holy mountain of God and walked among the stones of fire. "You were blameless in all you did from the day you were created until evil was found in you. And you sinned. So, I banished you in disgrace from the mountain of God. I expelled you, O mighty guardian, from your place among the stones of fire. Your heart was filled with pride because of all your beauty. Your love of splendor corrupted your wisdom. So, I threw you to the ground."*

All of the wonderful things that God created Lucifer with ended up getting him banished. His beauty, power, and wisdom activate his pride, which leads to his rebellion and, ultimately, his banishment. In God's grace, he never took away any of Satan's abilities, and with those abilities, he is leading a cosmic revolt against the creator and his creation. To this day, he can't see God's grace in his life.

The passage in Isaiah is directed to the 'King of Babylon,' and the Ezekiel passage is addressed to the 'King of Tyre.' But from the descriptions, it is clear that no human is addressed. The "I will" in Isaiah describes someone thrown to the earth as punishment for wanting to place his throne above the throne of God. The passage in Ezekiel addresses an 'angelic guardian' who once moved in Eden and the 'mountain of God.' Satan (or Lucifer) often puts himself behind or through someone else. In Genesis, he speaks through the serpent. In Isaiah, he rules through the King of Babylon, and in Ezekiel, he possesses the King of Tyre. Therefore, because evil or hate is all-consuming, it is easier to work from the top down to achieve the maximum effect.

To Steal

Satan feels like everything he deserves to have because

of who he is has been taken from him. Hence, he desires to cause this pain to God and us. Satan is not concerned about taking our jobs, even though he can use that kind of trauma to his benefit. He desires to steal our hope, our joy, our confidence in God, our peace, and, ultimately, our will to live. Most times, this is accomplished through earthly material and personal loss. Then, replace it with anger and hatred, setting us loose on the world.

To Kill

Satan's biggest target to kill in our lives is our hopes and dreams. A person who has no hope or the ability to dream of a better day is a person stuck in their past and, in most cases, their traumatic past. Many homeless individuals fall under this attack, but at the same time, many homeless people are suffering from legitimate chemical brain imbalances, so I do not want to place them all under this banner. However, those who are not, we live, walk, and drive among them daily. They moved to a different rhythm of life. There is little concern for personal hygiene, nor are they concerned about the same issues that concern you and me. They live for the moment, food, and shelter, and who can provide it for them through begging, panhandling, and/or crime?

The analogy here is not to focus on the homeless exclusively, but to use this current social and societal issue as a pictorial example of Satan's plan. While the homeless may reach the final stop, the question that should be asked is where they started from and what happened to them. What kills people's drive to believe, to have hope, to isolate, to withdraw, to feel unloved even by God? This is Satan's ultimate goal: to recruit an army of the angered and a congregation of the confused and set them loose to destroy themselves and others.

To Destroy

Destruction is never an action taken in isolation; it always has an underlying purpose. In most cases, it involves replacing something old with something new. In this so-called cosmic battle with God, we see Satan trying to pre-empt the born-again and new man process by destroying the natural things that are deeply connected to the youthful human spirit before that spirit can become an adult. To kill the process and keep the individual in an emotional and spiritual void of trauma through remembering past disappointments, pain, betrayals, jealousies, and envious friends and co-workers, and transferring those thoughts and emotions into their perspectives on how they see and interact with the world.

Satan's desire for God's creation is to get us so dissatisfied with our lives that our love will wax cold. Dissatisfaction with our careers through disappointments, dissatisfaction with our homes because we don't feel loved, respected, or relevant, lack of growth, and dissatisfaction with our children because we spoiled them, and now they are showing signs of ungratefulness, dissatisfaction with the world due to all the conflicts, how we treat each other, sexism, racism, misogyny, tribalism and those who fan these flames, and finally dissatisfied with God and his holy church, because the church looks identical to the world with its public displays of sins.

Dismantling the Demonic Design

The human psyche is fragile and highly vulnerable to the ebbs and flows of life. If delays or disappointments arise, the untrained mind gravitates toward negative thoughts. So, the key to dismantling Satan's attack is to be rooted and grounded in gratitude and humility. Below are three scriptures that lead us in this direction:

Deuteronomy 8:16-18, *"who fed you in the wilderness with manna, which your fathers did not know, that He might humble you and that He might test you, to do you good in the end then you say in your heart, 'My power and the might of my hand have gained me this wealth.'"*

Deuteronomy 8:18, *"And you shall remember the LORD your God, for it is He who gives you the power to get wealth, that He may establish His covenant which*

He swore to your fathers, as it is this day."

Philippians 4:6-7, *"Be anxious for nothing, but in everything by prayer and supplication, with thanksgiving, let your requests be made known to God; and the peace of God, which surpasses all understanding, will guard your hearts and minds through Christ Jesus."*

Approaching life from a position of humility, gratitude, and thanksgiving tends to dull the built-in hostility and resentment that the evil one so easily ignites in our hearts and then sends out to blame someone or something. This godly mindset transfers us from ownership of our lives to stewardship in our lives. This slight change in perspective enables us to see and believe that our lives do not belong to us, but have been given by God's grace, and we must conduct ourselves in a manner worthy of the gift that has been bestowed upon us.

As stewards, we are responsible for reporting to the giver of life all that is going right and wrong in our lives; as owners, we bear the responsibility to rectify all that is wrong in our lives and sustain all that is right. This is where Matthew 6:31-34 serves as a powerful antidote and a Satan killer, if appropriately applied to daily living: *"Therefore do not worry, saying, 'What shall we eat?' or 'What shall we drink?' or 'What shall we wear?' For after all these things, the Gentiles seek. For your heavenly Father knows that you need all these things. But seek God's kingdom and righteousness first, and all these things shall be added to you. Therefore, do not worry about tomorrow, for tomorrow will worry about its things. Sufficient for the day is its trouble."*

Capitalism: Satan's Playground

What makes the United States such an easy prey for Satan's schemes is that we are a double-minded society. We are a materialistic people with a capitalist mission while trying to live Judeo-Christian values. None of which are compatible with each other. James 1:6-8 says, *"But let him ask in faith, with no doubting, for he who doubts is like a wave of the sea driven and tossed*

by the wind. Let not that man suppose he will receive anything from the Lord; he is a double-minded man, unstable in all his ways.

This oxymoronic dynamic is played out daily in Western societies; it has been woven into the fabric of many countries globally. As the world becomes more industrious and interdependent on international trade for the survival of sovereign nations, we are witnessing an alarming increase in millionaires and billionaires around the globe. Global financial resources reside in the hands of a small percentage of the human population, with a meager amount trickling down to the middle classes.

This phenomenon sparks an increase in spending on goods and materialistic goods, such as luxury and high-performance vehicles, vacations, homes, jewelry, and designer clothes and accessories. A selfish and self-centered attitude of "I deserve these things" creeps into the human psyche, quickly followed by a need to downplay personal wealth and assets when confronted with financial disparities in the quality of living between people. These same folks will turn around and complain that governments need to do more to create safety nets for the vulnerable and that the rich need to pay more in taxes. This is the instability and double mindedness of the human psyche when a person realizes that they have been rooted in Satan's playground.

On the other end of the spectrum, we see the same selfish attitude on display, but this time, there are no such desires to hide or feel shame about the displaying and flaunting of obscene wealth in the faces of the poor and working poor masses. This group is not bound by morality but is instead motivated by greed and corruption, employing any means to maintain and acquire even more. In most cases, their methods always devastate families, kill careers, derail dreams, and create underclasses that, if not repressed by forces, will spark the seeds of revolution.

The question that must be asked is how people do not see the destruction they create. The apostle Paul gives us this answer very clearly:

2 Corinthians 4:4, *"whose minds the god of this age has blinded, who do not believe, lest the light of the gospel of the glory of Christ, who is the image of God, should shine on them."*

People choose Satan and his carnal earthly rewards because it is now and not eventually; this shows the limited faith people who value earthly power, prestige, and materialism have. The Bible calls him the god of this age because he controls the world's systems, not their economies, but the people who set the rules, behaviors, and requirements needed to succeed within his system. In this chapter, Paul also discusses the believer, their power, and its source.

2 Corinthians 4:7-9, *"But we have this treasure in earthen vessels, that the excellence of the power may be of God and not of us. We are hard-pressed on every side, yet not crushed; we are perplexed, but not in despair; persecuted, but not forsaken; struck down, but not destroyed."*

Satan's system is cruel, vicious, and brutal to all

who live because it taps into man's selfish desires for more. The greed for more deceives man into turning on others to eliminate competition. But those who trust in Christ and believe have something on the inside of their earthen bodies that is not of them; it is an excellent power source from above that will guarantee you never get crushed, fall into despair, left behind, or destroyed by anything this world system may come at you with. Satan's army only seems rich and powerful through the natural eye, but when you look at them through the spiritual eye, you have to pray for them, for they do not know what they are doing and which side they are on.

The Syrian king hunted the prophet Elisha, who sent a large army to capture him. When they caught up with him at night, they surrounded the hills of the city where he was staying, preparing to take him in the morning.

2 Kings 6:14-18, *"**Therefore, he sent horses and chariots and a great army there, and they came by night***

and surrounded the city. And when the servant of the man of God arose early and went out, an army surrounded the city with horses and chariots. And his servant said to him, "Alas, my master! What shall we do?" So, he answered, "Do not fear, for those who are with us are more than those who are with them." And Elisha prayed, saying, "Lord, I pray, open his eyes that he may see." Then the Lord opened the eyes of the young man, and he saw. And behold, the mountain was full of horses and chariots of fire all around Elisha. So, when the Syrians came down to him, Elisha prayed to the Lord and said, "Strike this people, I pray, with blindness." And he struck them with blindness according to the word of Elisha.

When we are in Satan's crosshairs, we can feel so alone, terrified, and defeated, but God always has a ram in the bush to protect his people, so pray that God touches your eyes so that you see that there are always more on your side than Satan's.

CHAPTER 10
A LOOK BACK

Jeremiah 5:21

*Hear this now, O foolish people,
without understanding, who have eyes and see not,
And who have ears and hear not.*

Combating Satan and his demonic designs always requires action on our part — a willing choice that leads to growth and improvement in our character. Honest reflection is vital to the process of healthy spiritual and emotional development.

As humans, we often stress ourselves to be perfect; we set expectations based on arrogance to support an unrealistic fantasy of manufactured happiness that cannot be attained or sustained. Then, we place these expectations on others with very neurotic and conservative attitudes. In this predicament, we often blame others for any failures we may experience in life's endeavors.

An example of this is a very lighthearted conversation I had with someone about a particular street intersection renovated in our home state of Texas. The design was different, and it was something we needed to become more familiar with. The state is following this design throughout its transportation system. But, in the middle of the conversation, the person blurted out, "It must be some progressives who did this." I thought about that statement for a while and wondered how someone could come to that conclusion. Who were the progressives, the construction workers, the subcontractors, and the Republican state government officials? Then it hit me: that comment was for me; it was a probing and investigative comment designed to elicit a favorable response that would provide approval and validation of how this person sees and experiences the world. I did not know this person intimately, nor am I familiar with their psychological pedigree; I could see their physical and cultural pedigree and assessed that they were seeing the world through a prewritten script of the American political ethos.

Eyes That Do Not See

We must recognize and reject the toxic theology that has infiltrated our hearts and society. This sin, camouflaged in the garb of Christendom, holiness, and righteousness, teaches us to focus on others' sins and misdeeds, fostering a narrative of victimhood. It is a narrative that justifies any response, even when it goes against the teachings of the scriptures. We must understand that bad behavior will corrupt good morals. Rejecting this sin paves the way for spiritual and emotional growth.

James 1:14-16, *"But each person is tempted when they are dragged away by their evil desire and enticed. Then, after desire has conceived, it gives birth to sin, and sin, when it is full-grown, gives birth to death. Do not be deceived, my dear brothers and sisters."*

James shows us the theology of internal temptation and the progressive nature of indwelling sin. When we live our lives in a point-counterpoint competitive manner, we become highly susceptible to being deceived by our desires and motivations; in other words, we become identical to what we condemn through our thoughts and desires. Jesus told us that not only is sin an insult to the Father, but also the thoughts of it.

The real problem at work here is the unnecessary nature of it all: the time wasted on independent rebellion to satisfy a sin-dominated ego when God himself has already given us his decrees and established them.

Divine Decree

A decree is an official order issued with the legal auth-ority to establish and guarantee its legitimacy. Our heavenly Father has established His Word in our hearts and deepened it in our consciousness. When this word is finally revealed to us from within, our behavior is modified. This is called transformation; the right transformation almost always leads to liberation if allowed.

Job 22:28, *"You will decide on a matter, and it will be established for you, and light will shine on your ways."*

Psalm 2:7 says, *"I will tell of the decree: The Lord said to me, 'You are my son; today I have begotten you."*

Romans 8:28, *"And we know that for those who love God all things work together for the good, for those who are called according to his purpose."*

Psalm 119:136, *"Incline my heart to your testimonies, and not to selfish gain."*

If the saints incline their hearts and ears to the Lord, all that is needed to fulfill their spiritual, emotional, and psychological lives will be met. This fulfillment produces the strength to reject sinful, cantankerous, and rebellious behavior in thought, speech, and deed among people. This process helps us remove the plank from our own eyes, rather than focusing solely on the specks in our neighbors'. Here is a radical shift in human psychology, which helps us control and conquer our sinful nature.

Satan and our sinful nature are dangerous to us in discovering our new man within. All sin is consuming and premeditative.

James 1:13-15, *"When tempted, no one should say, 'God is tempting me." God cannot be tempted by evil, nor does He tempt anyone; instead, each person is tempted when they are led astray by their evil desires and enticed. Then, after desire has conceived, it gives birth to sin, and sin, when it is full-grown, gives birth to death."*

This epistle begins by asking us to consider it a tremendous and joyous blessing when we encounter many trials. This testing and resisting produce perseverance and patience, which mature and complete us. We are fighting a very sophisticated form of warfare that will use our very desires against us and weaponize us to create destruction in our relationships, home, community, and country.

A Reflection of Gratitude

Those who believe in the Christian faith know that the God we serve is always ahead of us in our windshield and never behind us in our rearview mirror. This is why it takes strong faith in Him to move out towards Him rather than sit still in old victories.

Exodus 13:21, *"By day the LORD went ahead of them in a pillar of cloud to guide them on their way and by night in a pillar of fire to give them light so that they could travel by day or night."*

Our faith leads us physically, spiritually, and

emotionally; it always leads us. So, the question must be asked: Are we brave enough to follow God into the land he has created for us? Or will we continue to look back and serve those gods on the other side of the river? The deliverer, Joshua, asked the people the same question he had asked his people.

Joshua 24:13-15, *"So I gave you a land on which you did not toil and cities you did not build, and you live in them and eat from vineyards and olive groves that you did not plant. Now fear the LORD and serve him with all faithfulness. Throw away the gods your ancestors worshiped beyond the Euphrates River and in Egypt and serve the LORD. But if serving the LORD seems undesirable to you, choose for yourselves this day whom you will serve, whether the gods your ancestors served beyond the Euphrates or the gods of the Amorites, in whose land you are living. But for me and my household, we will serve the LORD."*

Joshua's statement in these verses reveals a too-familiar attitude toward God, which has led to an ungrateful spirit among the people. After all that had been given, they still were not satisfied with their lives because they were missing their familiar relationship with their sinful nature and all its competing, gossiping, lying, cheating, and stealing ways that brought a false sense of satisfaction to the soul.

Ungratefulness is the root of all sin, and pride is at the core of ungratefulness. Even though the children of Israel were worthy of deliverance from the bondage of the Egyptians, most were still an ungrateful nation. In the first three chapters of the Book of Romans, the apostle Paul describes this nature in detail. It is a universal condemnation of humanity and our sinful nature. He speaks of our many forms of sin, from coveting to malice, from our constant envy and jealousy to violent acts of murder, from gossip to slandering neighbors and coworkers, from hating God to disobeying our parents, from rebelliousness to self-righteousness, from doing evil to inventing evil, from the commission of sin to the approval of those who do it. This describes people in spiritual and emotional crises who are too ungrateful for what has been given and too prideful to honor and thank God for what He has done.

At its core, humanity has rejected God; we have dismissed him as creator, Lord, and ruler over all things in our world. With this rejection, we have replaced Him with self-worship, self-aggrandization, self-absorption, self-promotion, and self-consumption in everything from education to evangelizing, charity to greed, and love to lust.

Divine Right vs. Divine Law

What are divine rights? Do citizens of the earth have the right to apply the sacred rights of heaven on earth? When discussing divine rights, we refer to a right that may be interpreted as being bestowed by heaven to be exercised on earth, such as in the context of kingship. Many ancient European kingdoms were ruled under absolute divine authority; they were not theocracies but monarchies that believed they had a divine right to rule.

This came from their understanding of **Romans 13:1-5,** *"Let everyone be subject to the governing authorities, for there is no authority except that which God has established. God has established the authorities that exist. Consequently, whoever rebels against the authority is rebelling against what God has instituted, and those who do so will bring judgment on themselves. Rulers hold no terror for those who do right, but for those who do wrong. Do you want to be free from fear of the one in authority? Then do what is right, and you will be commended. For the one in authority is God's servant for your good. But if you do wrong, be afraid, for rulers do not bear the sword for no reason. They are God's servants, agents of wrath to bring punishment on the wrongdoer. Therefore, it is necessary to submit to the authorities, not only because of possible punishment but also because of conscience."*

What has been most concerning about this practice over the centuries is the many abuses perpetrated by said ruler over the citizenry, from the obscene number of wives and concubines to the acts of violence against wives and servants, murder, rape, pillaging, and unfairness that dominated daily life. So, compared to the divine right and the reality of daily practice, over the centuries, we see the hidden war within man and his nature versus the will of God.

Now, in comparison to divine rights, we have divine laws. What are divine laws? How are they to be interpreted and applied to daily living? Divine laws are moral and serve as a foundational standard of all righteousness for society. The most famous of the sacred laws is "The Ten Commandments." These ten laws define and shape our attitude toward God and our neighbors. The first four are our relationships with God, and the remaining six are our relationships with each other.

Ten Commandments: I am the Lord your God, who brought you out of the land of Egypt, out of the house of slavery.

- You shall have no other gods before me.

- You shall not make a carved image or likeness of anything in heaven above, in the earth beneath, or the water under the earth. You shall not bow down to them or serve them, for I, the Lord your God, am a jealous God visiting the iniquity of the fathers on the children to the third and fourth generation of those who hate me but showing steadfast love to thousands of those who love me, keep my commandments.

- You shall not take the name of the Lord your God in vain, for the Lord will not hold him guiltless who takes his name in vain.

- Remember the Sabbath day to keep it holy. Six days you shall labor, and do all your work, but the seventh day is a Sabbath to the Lord your God. You shall not do any work on it. You, or your son, or your daughter, your male servant, or your female servant, or your livestock, or the sojourner who is within your gates, for in six days the Lord made heaven and earth, the sea, and all that is in them and rested on the seventh day. Therefore, the Lord blessed the Sabbath day and made it holy.

- Honor your father and your mother. Your days may be long in the land the Lord your God is giving you.
- You shall not murder.
- You shall not commit adultery.
- You shall not steal.
- You shall not bear false witness against your neighbor.
- You shall not covet your neighbor's house, wife, male or female servants, ox or donkey, or anything else belonging to your neighbor.

It should be clear to all that the differences between presumed divine rights, which assume people were born with predetermined rights to rule others, and the conflict they create when compared to the sacred law of God are evident. As a community of believers in Christ, we need not look back to resurrect a sinful and divisive past, but rather learn from and correct past missteps, repent, and seek the forgiveness of God and one another.

Chapter 11

THE HEAVENLY VISION: RESTORATION OF THE WORLD

1 John 3:2-3

Beloved, now we are children of God, and it has not yet been revealed what we shall be, but we know that when He is revealed, we shall be like Him, for we shall see Him as He is. And everyone with this hope in Him purifies himself, just as He is pure.

The Highjacking of a Faith

John the Baptist announced a radical concept that came into the world. He called it the "Kingdom of God." Jesus announced this God-centered revolution to bring unity and harmony between God, humanity, and nature. It is called the "Good News" or "Gospels." It guides you through the Old Testament by exploring four foundational theologies, each highlighting a specific aspect of the infallible Word and its impact on a person's Christian faith.

1. Biblical Theology: This field examines how God's word has evolved and the diverse perspectives of biblical authors.
2. Historical or Dogma Theology: This field practices faith by paying particular attention to all movements of human history from the perspective of biblically informed views.
3. Systematic Theology: This field appropriates the theological voices of history through a canonical

perspective. It serves the church and God's people to live and act faithfully in accordance with God.
4. Practical Theology: This field practices the idea that all the behaviors and practices of the church and Christians are underwritten by theologies, which are biblical, historical, and systematic.

So, when claims are made about whom the faith favors more or that this is a Christian nation and all within its borders must submit to it, please understand that theology is a study of God's mind to help us become more like him in thought and deed. For this reason, we find in practical theology a sub-theology called liberation theology that comes from the prophet Isaiah's prophecy about Christ in **Isaiah 61: 1-3, *"The Spirit of the Lord God is upon me; because the Lord hath anointed me to preach good tidings unto the meek; he hath sent me to bind up the brokenhearted, to proclaim liberty to the captives, and the opening of the prison to them that are bound. To proclaim the acceptable year of the Lord,*** *and the day of vengeance of our GOD; To comfort all that mourn; To appoint unto them that mourn in Zion, to give unto them beauty for ashes, the oil of joy for mourning, the garment of praise for the spirit of heaviness; that they might be called trees of righteousness, the planting of the LORD, that he might be glorified."*

This theology is what is most needed to free God's Holy Church and its people from the grips of radicalism, nationalism, sectarianism, racism, and classism.

Liberation theology lives among the oppressed people of the world, those who are oppressed financially, socially, ethnically, spiritually, and by gender and race. It is a theology that addresses human activities such as greed, dominance, corruption, and the oppression and marginalization of individuals. This is a theology of internal revolution, constructing hopes and beliefs that transform people and how they perceive themselves beyond their circumstances. But more importantly, the theology of revolution identifies so closely with liberation theology because it is an internal theology against human indwelling sin. The prophet lists three things that Christ's mission came to help:

- The meek: Those who are submissive and endure wrongdoings
- The brokenhearted: Those who suffer from profound sadness and emotional distress due to deep loss and disappointment
- The captive: Those who are controlled by negative, unhealthy attachments through beliefs and behaviors.

What makes the Gospels so revolutionary is that they do not discriminate against people based on race, ethnicity, or financial status, but rather instruct us to help all based on their suffering. Meek, brokenhearted, and captive people can be found in America, Australia, New York, the Netherlands, Maine, and Mexico.

Liberation theology opposes the previously discussed dominion and reconstruction theologies. Unfortunately, these theologies are the most represented in the current rise of Christian nationalism due to people's disillusionment with big government, America's alleged moral decay, and the (alleged) failure of the "Great Society programs."[4]

Humanity

God desires that we do not conform to this sin-filled world but that we are transformed through a relationship with Jesus Christ. This relationship will purge the indwelling sin that plagues humanity, give sanction to evil, and coerce our complicit participation in the behavior. So, his desire is for us to become more like him through his son. This process requires a more profound commitment to communion with Him. Our divine mandate is to restore humanity by rescuing us from the powerful grip of sin that dwells within us. Our three main points of attack in this mission are:

---

[4] Paul Enns, The Moody Handbook Of Theology (Moody Publishers, 2014), 546

Faithfulness

Fruitfulness

Discipleship

Our faithfulness is priority number one, as it is the only way to overcome all discouragement, depression, and disappointments when the evil one begins to resist us through other sinful human beings. Our faith is required even unto death, for the scripture promises a better reward for our faithful service. Through faith, we are more than conquerors and overcomers.

Hebrews 11:30-40, *"By faith, the walls of Jericho fell after they were encircled for seven days. By faith, the harlot Rahab did not perish with those who did not believe when she had received the spies with peace. And what more shall I say? For the time would fail me to tell of Gideon and Barak and Samson and Jephthah, also of David and Samuel and the prophets: who through faith subdued kingdoms, worked righteousness, obtained promises, stopped the mouths of lions, quenched the violence of fire, escaped the edge of the sword, out of weakness were* *made strong, became valiant in battle, turned to flight, the armies of the aliens. Women received their dead raised to life again. Others were tortured, not accepting deliverance, that they might obtain a better resurrection. Still others had trials of mockery and scourging, yes, and of chains and imprisonment. They were stoned, they were sawn in two, they were tempted, and they were slain with the sword. They wandered about in sheepskins and goatskins, being destitute, afflicted, and tormented of whom the world was not worthy. They wandered in deserts and mountains, in dens and caves of the earth. And all these, having obtained a good testimony through faith, did not receive the promise, God having provided something better for us, that they should not be made perfect apart from us."*

Whenever we stand up to evil, we do so by faith and come in the name and full authority of Jesus Christ. Our faith and willingness to stand, speak, go, pray, give, and support to improve humanity gives us a better report in God's sight.

Another part of this vision is fruitfulness; we must grow and mature to multiply, not stagnate and disintegrate. We must recruit an army of change agents through discipleship. This mentorship process is best experienced through others who have witnessed your kindness, peace, calmness, thoughtfulness, and generosity. In most cases, it will be a completely new and foreign way of interacting for them. All human beings have a mandate from God to be fruitful in many ways while on the earth.

Genesis 1:26-28, *"Then God said, 'Let Us make man in Our image, according to Our likeness; let them have dominion over the fish of the sea, over the birds of the air, and over the cattle, over all the earth and over every creeping thing that creeps on the earth.' So, God created man in His image; in the image of God, He created him; male and female, He created them. Then God blessed them, and God said to them, 'Be fruitful and multiply; fill the earth and subdue it; have dominion over the fish* *of the sea, over the birds of the air, and over every living thing that moves on the earth."*

Our first mandate is to be fruitful in growing and multiplying the species through human reproduction. Human reproduction builds families, families build communities, and communities build nations. When examining biblical genealogy, we can see how fruitful it was in reproduction and how rapidly the Israelite nation expanded.

John 15:16, *"You did not choose Me, but I chose you and appointed you that you should go and bear fruit and that your fruit should remain, that whatever you ask the Father in My name He may give you.»*

Our second mandate is to be fruitful in good works, living according to Christ›s character. In this, we continue to cultivate God's creation through the expulsion of evil and the presence of ongoing brotherly love. Like human reproduction, this concept also reproduces in kind, as kindness begets kindness, charity begets charity, and compassion begets compassion. This is not always the case, but if done enough, the response can be so overwhelming that it can change a life, a family, a marriage, a student, and a ministry. The Holy Scriptures explain this in the Epistle to the Galatian Church:

Galatians 5:22-23, *"But the fruit of the Spirit is love, joy, peace, longsuffering, kindness, goodness, faithfulness, gentleness, self-control. Against such, there is no law."*

These nine human characteristics, displayed by us at different times as we go about our days, can be selectively applied to those we like or want to be around. However, they must be used not selectively but automatically as a primary way of living to be effective. We are called not to show partiality in the faith among the brethren. These characteristics cannot be selectively chosen to suit our preferences or abilities; they must be developed entirely within us for completeness in our character and spiritual life. This is the work of the Holy Spirit, to grow us in grace that others may experience the love and grace of the one who called us out of darkness.

We must look at the " Fruit of the Flesh " to show the contrast between God's vision for the restoration of his creation and man's desire to reshape God's creation according to his limited and selfish vision.

Galatians 5: 19-21, *"Now the works of the flesh are evident, which are: adultery, fornication, uncleanness, lewdness, idolatry, sorcery, hatred, contentions, jealousies, outbursts of wrath, selfish ambitions, dissensions, heresies, envy, murders, drunkenness, revelries, and the like; of which I tell you beforehand, just as I also told you in time past, that those who practice such things will not inherit the kingdom of God.*

As we compare the contrast between the characteristics, we see a glaring truth: our lostness and helplessness as a people to save ourselves from these all-consuming characteristics. But let us not get discouraged; all hope is not lost. These personality traits are natural and inherent; they have developed since birth and remain our primary responses to most situations and desires. But when we receive the promise of salvation and the knowledge of the spirit and his indwelling power, all that is required to reverse the onslaught of the flesh is a willingness and desire to change.

Many people cry out for God to intervene in their dire situations and circumstances after actively participating in those circumstances, and they fail to see and understand that they have been given the power to extricate themselves. By seeking and asking to be changed, God's power enables us to transform ourselves, and in doing so, our circumstances are altered, one person at a time.

Creation

The scriptures tell us that this planet belongs to God, for he is its creator and the owner of all that dwells on it.

Psalm 24: 1-2, *"The earth is the Lord's, and all its fullness, The world and those who dwell therein. For He has founded it upon the seas And established it upon the waters." Who may ascend into the hill of the Lord? Or who may stand in His holy place? He who has clean* *hands and a pure heart. Who has not lifted his soul to an idol, nor sworn deceitfully?*

With ownership, he has established specific requirements for those living on his property and wishing to enter his kingdom further. Requirements include the following—they must have:

- Clean hands: To live a life of righteousness, free from the guilt of wrongdoing and dishonesty
- Pure hearts: To confess sins through repentance and live obedient to God's word
- Lives not consumed by idol worship: Prioritize faith in God over idol consumptions of careers, relationships, and materialism
- Lives that have sworn in deceit: Prioritize honesty and integrity, and avoid false promises and falsehoods as a way to impress and get ahead

This is God's vision for humanity living on his creation and in harmony with nature: controlling, greed, letting go of comparing and competing with one another, building each other up spiritually and emotionally, and ultimately sustaining and looking out for each other on an individual, community, and international level.

We are all witnessing phenomena in the heavens that we have not seen or experienced before, particularly in relation to our weather and climate. These include smog ash clouds that shut down all flights in Europe for eight days in April 2010, massive cyclones in Japan, and the 2004 tsunami in the Indian Ocean that devastated Thailand. The recent superstorms have battered the United States' east and southern coastlines, the annual massive fires in the west and central parts of the U.S. and Australia, and earthquakes in India and Tibet. We are witnessing an increase in turbulent and life-threatening weather conditions that have occurred not gradually but rather suddenly. Global meteorological scientists agree that these conditions are linked to our selfish behavior of greed and opulence and our inability to adjust our lifestyles slightly, even when the evidence is apparent about our direction. Scripture speaks on this as well.

Genesis 1:28, *"Then God blessed them, and God said to them, 'Be fruitful and multiply; fill the earth and subdue it; have dominion over the fish of the sea, over the birds of the air, and over every living thing that moves on the earth."*

Man was given dominion over the living things on the earth to manage and care for, not to destroy them by destroying the earth's climate.

Genesis 2:15, *"Then the L*ORD *God took the man and put him in the garden of Eden to tend and keep it."*

God will hold man responsible for the damage he has done to the earth.

Revelations 11:18, *"The nations were angry, and Your wrath has come, And the time of the dead, that they should be judged, And that You should reward Your servants the prophets and the saints, And those who fear*

Your name, small and great, And should destroy those who destroy the earth."

Discipleship/Stewardship

The behavior of saints today reveals a severe lack of discipleship and stewardship within the Christian community. Christ Himself simplified the process of discipleship and stewardship within the body to two simple statements: "The Great Commandment and the Great Commission." Christ's disciples asked Him which commandment He considered the greatest, and His reply was revolutionary.

Matthew 22:36-40, *"Teacher, which is the great commandment in the law? Jesus said to him, 'You shall love the L*ORD *your God with all your heart, with all your soul, and with all your mind. This is the first and greatest commandment. And the second is like it: You shall love your neighbor as yourself. On these two commandments hang all the Law and the Prophets.'"*

This command was later followed by decisive action,

now known as "The Great Commission." After learning this, excellent command must be practiced as part of Christian daily living through witnessing and building unity among humanity through Godly love.

Unity Through Love

This powerful force draws people into a community and leads them to the foundational principles of forgiveness, selflessness, sacrificial actions, patience, and compassion.

- Forgiveness: God has forgiven us and expects us to forgive one another. **Ephesians 4:32,** ***"And be kind to one another, tenderhearted, forgiving one another, even as God in Christ forgave you."***
- Selflessness: God's selfless love is seen in the birth, life, and death of his son, Jesus Christ. **John 3:16,** ***"For God so loved the world that He gave His only begotten Son, that whoever believes in Him should not perish but have everlasting life."***
- Sacrificial: Jesus came into the world as a sacrificial

lamb for the cost of humanity's sinful rebellion against God. He said that no one can take his life, but he is willing to lay it down, for there is no greater love than that. **John 10:18,** ***"No one takes it from Me, but I lay it down of Myself. I have the power to lay it down, and I have the power to retake it. This command I have received from My Father."*** **John 15:13,** ***"Greater love has no one than this, than to lay down one's life for his friends."***

- Patience: The power of God's love is its ability not to get easily angered, resist hostility, and promote and display kindness. **1 Corinthians 13:4-8,** ***"Love is patient, love is kind. It does not envy, it does not boast, it is not proud. It does not dishonor others, it is not self-seeking, it is not easily angered, it keeps no record of wrongs. Love does not delight in evil but rejoices with the truth. It always protects, always trusts, always hopes, and always perseveres. Love never fails. But where*** *there are prophecies, they will cease; where there are tongues, they will be stilled; where there is knowledge, it will pass away."*

CONCLUSION

As this book comes to a close, it is essential to understand that the chapters have been laid out to illustrate a sweeping contrast between the Christian faith in its apostolic form and as a political movement.

The faith of Jesus Christ has always been designed to be a human organism and not a corporate organization. Organisms feel, connect, grow, develop, learn, and defend themselves. Organizations, even the ones that incorporate AI into their operating systems, often lack human empathy, feelings, kindness, sacrifice, and love for one another's well-being. Christianity can no more be a political party than a cow can lay an egg.

Christian nationalism is a myth. Nationalism is a real thing, but it cannot fall under the umbrella of Christianity, as nationalism is designed to be exclusive and not inclusive, and Christianity's call is to all who believe. The myth of Christian nationalism comes about because America has tried to tie Christianity to American patriotism by claiming it was founded as a Christian nation and culture and must be protected at all costs. But in reality, it is more deism in design, founded on the belief that it was created by a supreme being who established things so that all religions can be practiced peacefully without interference.

Americans believe that American culture must transform Christianity, while the Christian faith, which practices transforming lives, changes a culture. Either way, the Christian faith is under attack around the world by misguided saints who continue to believe in this perversion and are led by duplicitous leaders who exploit them for political and financial gain.

Even though our faith may be under attack, it does not necessarily mean our attackers will be successful in their quest as long as the church stays diligent in its doctrine and faithful in its commitment.

My closing message to the faithful is, as always:

Ephesians 5:15-16, *"See then that you walk circumspectly, not as fools but as wise, redeeming the time, because the days are evil."*

BIBLIOGRAPHY

Ennis, Paul. *The Moody Handbook of Theology*. Chicago, IL: Moody Publishers, 2014.

Rosner, Brian S. *Known By God*. Grand Rapid, MI, Harper Collins, 2017.

Packer, J. I. *Knowing God*. Downers Grove, IL, InterVarsity Press, 1973.

Williams, Owen. *American Christianity: Black Liberation White Legalism.* Pflugerville, TX, Grapevine, 2023.

Williams, Owen. *The Corporate Christian III: The Hidden War.* Pflugerville, TX, Grapevine, 2023.

MORE ABOUT PASTOR WILLIAMS

Pastor Owen E. Williams is the Pastor of St. Mark Missionary Baptist Church and the retired Director of Pastoral Care Services at Kings County Medical Center.

Pastor Williams has a Bachelor of Science degree in Administrative Planning in Criminal Justice and Criminology, a master's degree in Christian Ministry and Pastoral Counseling, an Honorary Doctorate in

Christian Ministries, and is a graduate of the New York City Police Department Citizens Academy.

Pastor Williams is the President of the Queens Federation of Churches Board of Directors, a board member emeritus of Live on NY, a member emeritus of the 103rd Precinct Executive Community Board, a member of the Clergy Liaison Staff for the 103rd Precinct, and a member of the Committee for Religious Liberties in Washington, DC. The founder and president of O.E. Williams Ministries is a non-profit organization with a footprint in Johannesburg, South Africa.

At St. Mark Missionary Baptist Church, he has established numerous ministries and conducted workshops on deaconship, mission work, and ushering, both within and outside the church. He built a phenomenally successful outreach ministry, which included vacation Bible school, book bag and backpack giveaways, clothing and food pantries, healthcare, and social services. He has also established OE Williams Ministries in South Africa, conducting semiannual certification training for social workers, schoolteachers, crisis counselors, police officers, and clergy on "Solution-Focused Pastoral Counseling."

At Kings County Medical Center, he was responsible for an Ecumenical Ministry that served the spiritual needs of over 600 patients and 5,000 staff. He created an extensive community outreach program, a lay chaplain volunteer program, and grief counseling services for patients, family members, and staff. He also oversaw the spiritual council for the entire system of eleven acute care hospitals.

He is the author of four published books:

The Corporate Christian: Christian Beliefs vs. Corporate Behaviors

The Corporate Christian II: The Battle for Your Beliefs

The Corporate Christian III: The Hidden War

American Christianity: Black Liberation White Legalism

Pastor Williams has been married to Elder Debora Williams for 35 years, and they have one daughter, Desiree Rose Williams.

www.ingramcontent.com/pod-product-compliance
Lightning Source LLC
Chambersburg PA
CBHW070627030426
42337CB00020B/3944